N Gauge Modelling

An Introductory Guide

by HOWARD FOY

Engee Publishing
Prestwich, Manchester, M25 3AE

Published by
Engee Publishing
16 Dashwood Road
Prestwich
Manchester, M25 3AE

Tel: 07940-802336
e-mail: howardefoy@yahoo.co.uk

British Library Cataloguing In Publication Data
A catalogue record for this book is available from the British Library

For Kate and Daisy D

ISBN: 978-0-9560943-0-8

Typeset, Designed and Produced by
Engee Publishing

Printed by
Rap Spiderweb Ltd
Clowes Street
Hollinwood
Oldham
Lancashire
OL9 7LY

CONTENTS

Foreword

COMMERCIAL modelling of British railways in N Gauge is now around 40 years old. Whether you take the anniversary as being 2007, the 40th birthday of the founding of the N Gauge Society – and 40 years exactly since Peco produced their first ready-made N Gauge wagons – or perhaps 2010, four decades since the year Graham Farish announced the launch of their first N Gauge "Masterpieces in Miniature", this seems an opportune moment to commemorate and celebrate the milestone with the publication of a book dedicated solely and specifically to modelling in 2mm scale.

N Gauge Modelling: An Introductory Guide is not the first book to be devoted to the scale in the UK since the late 1960s. But it seems somewhat surprising that a trawl of archives and the Internet could turn up only two other specific publications which have appeared in the past 40 years – *N Gauge Model Railways* by Michael Andress (Almark Publications) back in 1972 and *Micro-Model Railways* by Stephen Kelly (David and Charles) 10 years later in 1982 – both of which are, inevitably, now long out of print and well out of date.

With N Gauge in the UK undoubtedly going from strength to strength as the Noughties unfold, it is felt that a new publication such as this is long overdue. It is not intended to supplant the many excellent general books on railway modelling that have been published in recent years. On the contrary, several of these publications are mentioned and recommended in the text.

But it is undoubtedly a frustrating fact for N Gauge devotees that the

FIRST STEPS . . . The Graham Farish Freight Starter Set   *(Pic: Graham Farish)*

many general modelling books usually cast only a cursory glance over the 2mm scene while concentrating on modelling in the (admittedly more popular) 00 Gauge. General books – and the many excellent monthly magazines, for that matter – also have to find space for other scales and modes of modelling from Z Scale through narrow-gauge formats such as 009 to 0 Gauge and beyond.

It is, thus, the intention in the following pages to give newcomers to the hobby and/or to the scale an overview of what N Gauge modelling is all about and to provide some practical advice and information about how to proceed. The book covers N Gauge-specific help on choosing an era, style and configuration of layout as well as more general matters such as space considerations, laying track, prpvioding the electrics and building the scenery – but all with an N Gauge bias.

These chapters are not intended to be comprehensive and, where necessary, the reader will be given signposts pointing where to turn for more specialised advice. But anyone of whatever age who is contemplating an N Gauge layout for the first time – or for that matter, looking for ways to expand and develop their modelling in the scale – should find much valuable information in the following pages to help them get a project under way.

Happy reading – and happy modelling!

Howard Foy, Autumn 2008

SCALE AND GAUGE

TO the modelling newcomer, the jargon and terminology associated with railways, both full size and in model form, can seem both complex and confusing. In everyday usage, the terms "scale" and "gauge" have become blurred and their precise meanings somewhat mixed up.

Strictly speaking, **GAUGE** – when applied to both full-size and model railways – is a measurement of the distance between the inside faces of two rails of track. In the real thing, Standard Gauge, which applies to most major railway systems around the world, is 4ft 8.5in, while in modelling terms, N Gauge is 9mm.

SCALE, as used in the modelling sense, refers to the ratio of the size of a model compared to its full-size prototype. An N Gauge model of a British locomotive, coach or wagon which is said to be to a scale of 1:148 is thus one-148th the size of the real thing.

To put it another way, a real-life item which is one foot long would be a one-hundred and forty-eighth of a foot long in N Gauge model form – roughly 2mm. Hence the 1:148 ratio can also be expressed in modelling terminology as 2mm to the foot – that is, 2mm on the model equals (approximately) one foot on the prototype.

Throughout the history of railway modelling, and, hence, in the context of this book, both N Gauge and 2mm (scale) have become interchangeable terms for model railway systems using track with a gauge of 9mm, but there are marked differences between the 1:148 scale of models in British outline and the 1:160 scale of models of European and other foreign rail systems.

There is one other important point to note about modelling jargon. The mixing of metric and imperial measures in this terminology, such as 2mm to the foot, is not intended to confuse – it is just the way the terms have developed over the years and how they are used in most UK modelling literature.

Here's a simple glossary of the terms used in this book:

N GAUGE is the universal shorthand term for models of main-line rail systems running on track with a 9mm width between the rails. N was chosen in the early commercial days of the hobby because the word "nine" starts with that letter in most major languages. In North America, the term normally used is **N SCALE**.

2mm SCALE is an alternative shorthand term for N Gauge because, as a general guide, 2mm on a model roughly equates to 1ft on the real thing. In the same way, 00 gauge can be referred to as 4mm (to the foot) and 0 Gauge as 7mm. To be strictly exact, 1:148 scale actually equals 2.06mm to the foot, and 1:160 scale is 1.91mm to the foot.

9mm is the measurement of the distance between the inside edges of the rails on N Gauge track. In 1:160 scale this equates almost exactly to standard gauge track.

In the British variant of 1:148, the track equivalent is actually 4ft 4.5in – and to be strictly exact, 1:148 stock should run on track with a width of 9.7mm.

1:148 SCALE refers to the ratio of the size of the model of a British-outline N Gauge model in comparison to the full-size prototype. This means that a model of, say, a Duchess Pacific, a Class 66 diesel or any other type of UK loco or rolling stock. is one-148th the size of the real thing.

1:160 SCALE refers to the ratio of the size of a model of a European and North American N Gauge loco or item of rolling stock to the real thing. The dichotomy between 1:148 and 1:160 is explained in Chapter 2 and is a consequence of the differing Loading Gauges of the different railway systems.

1:150 SCALE refers to the ratio of the size of Japanese N Gauge locos and rolling stock (except "bullet trains") to the real thing, based on the original 3ft 6in gauge of most Japanese railways.

1:152 SCALE is the ratio adopted by the 2mm Association in the UK for specialist finescale modelling with a track gauge of 9.42mm which equates almost exactly to 4ft 8.5in.

000 (Treble-Oh) is the term given to models of roughly 2mm to the foot scale running on 9mm – originally 8.5mm – track by scratchbuilders from the 1920s onwards and commercially by Lone Star for their range of push-along and electric trains in the late 1950s and early 1960s. The designation fell out of use with the demise of the Lone Star range and the adoption, firstly in Europe, of N Gauge as the universal 2mm term.

STANDARD GAUGE is the term used worldwide for railways with a track width of 4ft 8.5in as adopted in the UK from the pioneering days of the Stockton & Darlington in 1825, and subsequently by most railways in Europe and North America, on which the N Gauge 9mm model standard is based. Other systems in use around the world – which we can largely ignore for N Gauge modelling purposes – use broad gauge track of 5ft or 5ft 6in, metre gauge (3ft) or narrow gauge.

LOADING GAUGE is the term used for the maximum dimensions of rolling stock in terms of width and height. In the UK, the loading gauge has a maximum height of 13.5ft and a maximum width of around 9ft for locos and rolling stock. Abroad, loading gauges are more generous. It is the difference between loading gauges which led to the difference in scale between UK and foreign N Gauge stock.

FINESCALE, in British-outline 2mm terms, refers to the specialist hobbyists who model in 1:152 scale.

PROTOTYPE is the term for the full-sized original on which a model is based. It can refer both to individual locos, items of rolling stock or structures and to the railway system as a whole.

RTR is the shorthand term for ready-to-run rolling stock ie. Commercially-produced items which can go straight out of the box and on to the track.

SCRATCHBUILDING is the term for constructing items of rolling stock or scenery from basic raw materials, self-made components or ready-made objects converted from other uses – for experienced modellers only!

DCC stands for Digital Command Control, a system of operating model railways using computer chips and decoders instead of conventional two-rail block wiring.

1 Introduction

WHETHER you are new to railway modelling or are contemplating a change of scale for space reasons, the question you will be asking as you pick up this book is a simple one: Is N Gauge the right scale for me?

It is a question that many thousands of modellers have asked themselves over the past 40 years or so, and it is one that *N Gauge Modelling: An Introductory Guide* aims to answer.

The first years of the new millennium have seen N Gauge in the UK enjoying a welcome surge in popularity, and the quality and range of ready-to-run British-outline models now on offer from Graham Farish, Dapol, Peco and specialist firms make the scale – at long last – a viable alternative option to 00 for serious modelling of the UK scene both past and present. Indeed, it is not too far-fetched to suggest that N Gauge in its British guise is entering a "golden age" that will make it a serious rival for 00 in the years to come.

This resurgence was undoubtedly sparked by Bachmann's takeover of the one long-established British-outline N Gauge manufacturer, Graham Farish, in the summer of 2000, and was given a big boost by the arrival of Dapol as a serious N Gauge manufacturer in 2003.

In 2006 we saw Peco re-entering the field as a loco supplier and more recently Australian newcomers Ixion launched their own magnificent GWR Manor locomotive in association with Dapol – with the promise of more to come. Mention should also be made here of the continuing availability of "bespoke" N Gauge locos and rolling stock from specialist traders like Union Mills, CJM, Ian Stoate and Millfield Models.

The most pressing reason why modellers consider N Gauge is obviously the question of space. Limits on available room to pursue the modelling hobby – especially in modern houses – often mean that N Gauge is the only scale worth serious consideration if you want a layout in which trains run from Point

PUSH AND PULL . . . Lone Star's 000 trains ran on 9.5mm track   *(Pic:Adam Foy)*

A to Point B or where you want to see your models operating in a generous continuous run in an authentic miniature landscape.

But space isn't the only factor that points the way to 2mm for many modellers. There are probably as many different reasons for choosing N Gauge as there are types of N gauge layout that can be planned, built and enjoyed. It may be that you saw a particular N gauge layout at an exhibition, or in one of the monthly railway modelling magazines, or perhaps it was a favourite locomotive running in the scale at a show, or featured in an advertisement, that caught your eye.

In this writer's case, it was a display of original push-pull Lone Star 000 toys in a shop window that proved entrancing at the age of eight or nine. At that time – around 1960 – 00 model trains in the form of Tri-ang and Hornby Dublo were becoming increasingly popular toys and in due course a Tri-ang 00 Princess Elizabeth loco, a couple of carriages and an oval of track were a welcome Christmas present as interest in model railways grew.

But there was never enough room at home to keep the train set out for long – let alone build a layout – and interest inevitably waned as school, exams, football (and girls!) began to take precedence as the teenage years progressed.

In the early 1960s – as we will see in Chapter 2 – serious 2mm scale modelling was still very much in its infancy, and with Lone Star's decline and demise from the middle of the decade, there were few commercial products available and little interest from the modelling press to keep an interest in the scale alive.

But it was impossible to forget the impact of that first view of a 000 window display, and when Graham Farish and Hornby Minitrix launched into British N Gauge in the early 1970s, there was only ever one serious scale to contemplate as a railway modeller.

Whatever your reasons for choosing N Gauge, the inescapable fact of 2mm

MINIATURE LANDSCAPE . . . Littlewood, the magnificent layout created by N Gauge master craftsman Richard Deas and on the exhibition circuit 1999-2002, shows how impressive a 2mm scale panorama can be if space and skill are seemingly no object!

modelling is, of course, the small size of the models. N Gauge track, at a gauge – the width between the rails – of nine millimetres, is almost exactly half the size of 00's 18.5mm, but the actual difference in linear scale between the two formats is twice that. In other words, an N Gauge layout will take up just one-quarter of the space of an identical layout in 00.

This is a huge advantage if the principal aim of a layout is to see trains running through a realistic landscape with a near-prototypical number of carriages or wagons, or the desire is to create a complex design of trackwork such as a busy junction or main-line station.

Where a 00 gauge layout might feature a station and a short section of track inside a narrow strip of scenery before disappearing into a tunnel or burrowing behind a backscene, the same space in N Gauge allows for realistic sections of miniature landscape to be created. Train lengths, too, can be more realistic. An eight-coach train in N Gauge, for instance, is roughly the same length as a four-coach train in 00 – although it only occupies around half the width and a quarter of the height.

The principal drawback is that some modellers may feel that N gauge is just

HERE COMES THOMAS . . . another busy scene on Richard Deas' Littlewood layout showing the panoramic effect that can be achieved in N Gauge where space permits

too small to work in – particularly if you are new to the hobby and your skills are, of necessity, somewhat limited.

It was certainly true in the early days that much skill and aptitude was needed for serious modelling in N Gauge, when the range of ready-to-run items was limited and intricate kit-building of both locomotives and rolling stock and scenic elements was the only way to construct a realistic 2mm scale layout. Indeed, the early days of the hobby in the 1970s often demanded scratchbuilding for any layout not covered by the limited range of RTR products available at that time.

But that is certainly no longer the case. The re-launched Graham Farish range from Bachmann from 2001 onwards and the N Gauge products offered by Dapol cover most area of postwar British railways in steam, diesel and 25kv electric very well and there is a selected coverage of steam locos and rolling stock in the liveries of the Big Four to permit reasonably accurate layouts covering the 1923-48 period as well.

And it is now possible to purchase many N Gauge scenic items ready-made and ready-painted, such as the wide-ranging Lyddle End accessories from Hornby and the splendid new Scenecraft range from Bachmann-Graham Farish. This means it is easy and relatively cheap to put together a complete N Gauge townscape or industrial facility – not to mention much of the actual lineside infrastructure – without so much as looking at a craft knife or paintbrush.

As mentioned above, the principal advantage of N Gauge is that where space is not at a premium it can be possible to build a layout on which to run decent-length main-line trains in an environment in which a much broader segment of countryside or townscape can be effectively reproduced. The one-quarter size

LITTLE WONDER . . . The station building and associated modules produced by Bachmann in their new Scenecraft range of ready-built N Gauge buildings

OVERHEAD ANGLE . . . two prototype-length goods trains pass through Littlewood station, while on a lower level diesels come on and off a busy depot

compared to 00 means that some of the finer details of modelling are inevitably lost, particularly with locomotives and rolling stock. But even in this area, the much-improved quality of models these days – in terms of things like lining and signage and the more intricate aspects of liveries – can bear comparison with the larger scales.

Another important point to bear in mind, when considering whether N Gauge is the right scale for you, is to be clear about how you want to observe and enjoy a 2mm scale layout. It is just about possible to get the eye-line down to almost rail level with 00 to watch trains going past as if you are trainspotting from the lineside or platform end. But this is impossible with the smaller scale.

No matter how you try to keep the eye focused on a 2mm model – whether it is moving or stationary – the brain will register the smaller size and keep it at a greater distance than its 00 equivalent. Try zooming in with the naked eye as if looking through a camera lens and at a certain point the view will start to blur. Only with the aid of a magnifying glass can true close-up views be achieved.

Inevitably, N Gauge layouts and trains are best viewed from an overhead aspect – as if you are observing from a tall building, a hillside or a helicopter. But this is the true joy of modelling in 2mm.While N Gauge lacks the finer details of the larger scales in which you can imagine yourself going INTO the model and becoming part of the action, it is the ideal scale to appreciate and enjoy the overall picture of railway operation in the landscape.

If you feel that watching the trains go by from a lineside perspective is one of the most important aspects of modelling, then N Gauge is probably not the scale for you. Anyone with any doubts about this aspect of the hobby should make a point of seeing and comparing N Gauge and 00 layouts at an exhibition before taking the plunge.

One final aspect of N Gauge modelling which it is important to bear in mind is the cost. The models may be 75% smaller than their 00 equivalents but that difference is unfortunately not reflected in the prices. In fact, commercially-available locomotives and some items of rolling stock can sometimes be a bit more expensive than similar items in 00.

This is not really surprising as it must be remembered that these are precision models and the initial setting-up costs and manufacture are much the same as for the larger scale. While N Gauge models obviously use less metal or plastic in their construction, the overall costs of castings and body mouldings are similar or indeed higher, given the greater intricacies involved, and the number of moving parts is roughly the same in any scale. Also the process of manufacturing and assembling these miniature masterpieces can take even longer.

And on the subject of cost, many more locomotives and items of rolling stock can be accommodated on N Gauge layouts than on 00 layouts of similar overall dimensions. It is probably inevitable that the temptation will be there to add more and more stock – so modelling in the smaller scale can actually work out much more expensive in the long run!

FINE DETAILS . . . The Graham Farish Freightliner 100-tonne HHA Bogie Hopper Wagon shows up well the intricate finish and signage on today's N Gauge models (GF)

15

2 Why N Gauge?

SO what exactly do we mean by the term "N Gauge"? How was the scale born and how has it developed into the wide-ranging network of models – covering almost all British, European, North American and Japanese railway systems – available to us today?

Before we go any further, it should perhaps be pointed out that "N" is by no means a universal scale with a universal meaning. What we recognise as N in the UK is not what is normally accepted by modellers in the rest of the world. Even within the British modelling fraternity, there is a marked division between those who prefer to model European or North American N in 1:160 scale – that is, 1 inch (or centimetre) on the model equates to 160 inches (or centimetres) on the real thing – and the rest who model British outline in the slightly larger 1:148 scale. And we must also mention the purists who model UK and other railways in 2mm finescale, which actually equates to 1:152.

Forty years or so ago, when N Gauge was in its infancy in Britain, there was a major debate between the various camps as attempts were made to establish a set of common rules and standards for 2mm modelling which would be acceptable to all. For historical reasons which also apply to the 00/H0 division, unity was never going to be possible – and it is perhaps inevitable that for newcomers to N Gauge, confusion still exists to this day.

To explain why and how this odd state of affairs came about, a brief history of the railway modelling hobby is probably necessary. So let's begin at the beginning.

Models of trains are almost as old as the real thing. Certainly, within 30 years of the celebrated opening of the world's first true passenger-carrying railway, the Liverpool and Manchester, in 1830, toymakers in both Europe and North America were creating tinplate clockwork models that were rough

FIRST IN THE WORLD . . The Liverpool & Manchester Railway opened in 1830 (DCS)

facsimiles of real locomotives and rolling stock of those pioneering days. The history books record documentary evidence of a model steam loco being built in Britain as early as 1833, and also a possible model railway constructed in a garden setting for an exhibition by Leeds Mechanical Institute in 1838.

The eminent railway historian C Hamilton Ellis, in his 1962 book *Model Railways 1839-1939,* talks of a clockwork train made in Forestville, Connecticut, in the US in 1856 and apparently a German toymaker was producing similar examples from a factory in the Black Forest at around the same time. In Britain, Ellis's researches unearthed evidence of a pioneering clockwork toy loco called Grace produced by a London clockmaker in 1867.

The late Victorian era saw several toy manufacturers in Britain and Europe producing tinplate clockwork trains for well-to-do children, while examples of cheaper pull-along and push-along wooden models survive in toy museums around the country.

Victorian railway models were usually freelance designs of indeterminate scale and track gauge, but even the smallest examples produced were rarely smaller than a size we would recognise today as 0 Gauge or more likely the larger (garden railway-sized) Gauge 1.

Developments in tinplate manufacture in the final decade of the 19th Century allowed German toymakers including Marklin and Bing to offer the very first model railway systems, with roughly to-scale versions of locomotives and rolling stock plus track, signals and rudimentary accessories. However, being 0 Gauge or bigger, these were not the sort of models you would find in the

*SETTING STANDARDS . . . **Model Railways and Locomotives**, first published in 1909, set out the first specifications for railway modelling gauges in the UK*

average household, and their size meant that they were not suited to the creation of permanent table-top layouts.

It was Bing in 1891 which first attempted to lay down a series of standard sizes, or gauges, for their railway models, powered by both clockwork and steam, and they came up with No 1 Gauge, based on a track width of 1.75in, No 2 Gauge (2in) and No 3 Gauge (2.75in). There was even originally a No 4 Gauge with a track width of 3.5in.

Meanwhile in Britain, *Model Railways and Locomotives* magazine, the pioneering "bible" of the hobby, was first published in January 1909, and it was an article in an early issue of that magazine saw the first attempt to standardise these model dimensions to be followed by manufacturers of tinplate clockwork and live-steam models and the early scratchbuild hobbyists alike.

Taking Bing's system as its basis, it was that article which effectively laid down for UK modellers the nomenclature of model railway scales which are so familiar to us today with a first written description of the dimensions of 0 Gauge – although that was the smallest scale listed therein. With a track gauge of 32mm and a scale of 7mm to the foot, it is known universally today in its spoken form as Oh-Gauge. But that derivation was originally ZERO-Gauge as it was smaller than the progressively-larger Gauges 1, 2 and 3.

It should perhaps be said at this point, however, that most pioneer hobbyists before 1914 indulged in model railways, but not true railway modelling. This is not just a question of semantics. The former term covers the construction and/or operation of scale models of locos or rolling stock, while the latter encompasses a system, or layout, which brings together those two elements with track and scenic items such as stations, bridges, tunnels and landscape elements in a permanent or semi-permanent formation.

For the former to become the latter in an indoor setting, it was necessary for there to be a development of a scale smaller than 0 Gauge. That scale, half the size of 0, and with a track gauge which was later defined as 16.5mm, is what became known as H0 (half-Oh) in Europe and North America and 00 (double-Oh) in the UK.

The breakthrough came in 1921 when the German firm Bing officially launched the first H0 clockwork train sets running on track with a width of 16.5mm and with vehicles built to a scale of 3.5mm to the foot. A couple of years later, the first British prototypes appeared from the German firm, working in conjunction with the UK model firm of Bassett-Lowke – first in clockwork and then a year later with a rudimentary form of electric control.

In Germany, other manufacturers including Marklin and Trix jumped on the bandwagon, although the difficult economic times following the First World War meant these were exclusive products available only to the very rich.

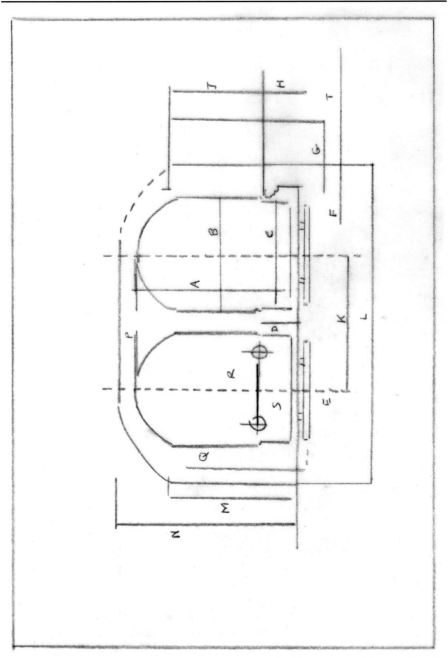

VITAL STATISTICS . . . This complex system of lines and letters (roughly reproduced) is a technical description of the UK loading gauge and sets maximum dimensions of rolling stock and minimum height of bridges and widths of track formations

From the outset, however, there was an unavoidable problem with H0 which was replicated 30 years later with the birth of N Gauge. This is the fact that the LOADING GAUGE adopted by British railways is somewhat smaller than that adopted by railway systems in most areas of the rest of the world – particularly Europe and North America.

Some clarification may be welcome here, particularly for readers who are not over-familiar with railway jargon. "Loading gauge" is not the same thing as track gauge or the use of the latter word as applied to models.

Britain, of course, pioneered the railways, and – with the notable exception of Brunel's broad gauge Great Western – they were immediately regularised on a uniform 4ft 8.5in track width with a maximum height of 13.5 ft and a maximum width of around 9ft for locos and rolling stock. These dimensions are crucially important because the construction of the entire railway network, in terms of stations, bridges, tunnels and track layouts, are dependent on them, and it is this collection of figures which is known as the *loading gauge.*

In Europe and North America, most railways also adopted 4ft 8.5in track, but the more open spaces elsewhere in the world allowed foreign companies to run wider and taller trains on this track – and hence they have a markedly bigger loading gauge. In Europe, trains can be 14ft high and 10ft wide, while in the wide-open spaces of North America on most lines they can run rolling stock which is 15ft high and 10.5ft wide. And this is where the modelling dichotomy comes into play.

Scaled down to 3.5mm to the foot and running on 16.5mm track, models of foreign trains are designated H0 (half-Oh) because their basic dimensions are roughly 50% of the comparable dimensions of 0 Gauge. But as the British loading gauge is smaller than elsewhere, models of British outline locomotives built to the same H0 scale would be too small to accommodate the drive mechanisms as originally developed for foreign locos.

The problem was solved by Henry Greenly, a pioneer of model and miniature railways in the 1920s who was one of the driving forces behind the design and construction of the 15-inch gauge Romney, Hythe & Dymchurch Railway in Kent. As a consultant to the Bassett-Lowke model company, he suggested that they should keep the H0 track gauge of 16.5mm but make the bodywork to a slightly larger scale so that Continental drive mechanisms would fit inside. Hence 00 was born.

This became the standard for British-outline models in the 1930s when first Trix Trains and then Meccano, with the launch of Hornby Dublo, offered complete train sets in 4mm scale with track and accessories. The latter advertised their products as "the Perfect Table Railway".

To the average table-top hobbyist, this difference is so small as to be almost insignificant unless you put European and British stock side-by-side, although for the purists modelling in 4mm, more specialist and largely scratchbuilt parallel systems now exist, including EM and P4.

The widespread acceptance and popularity of 00 from the 1960s onwards was undoubtedly a result of the scale's dual function – 00 models are not too big to go on a table-top and not too small to have a double life as both playthings for growing children as well as the basis of serious model layouts for aficionados of all ages.

But of course, the story doesn't stop there. Trends in design and manufacture down the years, from computers to home appliances and mobile phones, has been one of miniaturisation. The drive has been to make all things smaller if possible – and it was inevitable that model railways would be no different.

So just as 0 Gauge was halved in size and track gauge to become 00, there was from the 1930s onwards a drive to halve those 00 dimensions too, and hence N Gauge – or 000 as it was originally known – was born.

In the late 1950s, the first attempt at a smaller commercial system than 00 was TT as launched by Tri-ang in Britain and a couple of manufacturers abroad. The initials stood for "Table-Top" and it was based on a track gauge of 12mm and a scale of 2.5mm or 3mm to the foot. A range of scaled-down variants of Tri-ang's 00 models and accessories was launched, but somehow TT never really took off.

At around the same time the first commercial developments in what would become the N Gauge story were stirring – in the unlikely guise of an engineering firm based in north London called Die Casting Machine Tools Ltd with a range of push-along toys under the Lone Star brand.

Historically speaking, a small band of dedicated railway modellers began scratchbuilding locomotives and rolling stock to a rough approximation of 2mm to the foot as early as the 1920s, on a track gauge which became standardised at 9.5mm. One of these pioneers, H.B. Whall – who later became the first president in 1960 of the 2mm Association – even built a layout with two working locomotives. And in 1927, a working model of a Midland Railway Johnson 0-6-0 locomotive in 2mm apparently ran successfully at a model exhibition in Wimbledon, south-west London.

After the Second World War, H.B. Whall took advantage of his retirement to set up a small business making a range of 2mm parts and some finished models for like-minded hobbyists, who began adopting the nomenclature of 000 (Treble-Oh) as their chosen scale's designation. Indeed, interest in the scale had grown to such an extent that a book devoted to the subject, *Modelling In 000 Gauge*, was written by pioneer hobbyist E.F. Carter in 1955.

It wasn't the efforts of expert modellers like H.B. Whall which kick-

000 LOCOS . . . Lone Star's push-along Stanier Princess Royal in blue, BR 2-6-4 tank and silver Gresley A4 were rough approximations of the real thing   *(Pic: Adam Foy)*

started commercial production of 000, however, but the somewhat surprising intervention of a metal-bashing company in North London looking to diversify into toy production after the Second World War.

Die Casting Machine Tools Ltd (DCMT), was a company which originally specialised in die-casting of zinc and other metal alloy products at their factory in Palmers Green. In the early 1950s, they started manufacturing die-cast metal "Wild West" toys such as cap-guns and pistols under the Lone Star brand name. They soon branched out into other die-cast toys including boats and cars.

In 1957, DCMT, now re-located to Hatfield in Hertfordshire, launched Lone Star Trains as a push-along range of toys roughly half the size of 00 and running on 8.25mm track – exactly 50% of the larger scale – and advertised as 000 gauge. The models were sold as gift sets and as individual models and ran to more than 40 items of rolling stock and lineside accessories such as telegraph poles and fencing.

Six locos were available, including models based on the Gresley A4 and Stanier Princess Royal Pacifics, plus two tank engines and a North American "Transcontinental" diesel. It has to be said that these were only rough approximations of the real thing, as were the rudimentary coaches and goods stock, with simple pin-and-loop couplings and one-piece wheel sets. But as these items were designed purely as toys for young children, prototypical accuracy was never intended to be a priority.

In Europe, the German firm Trix of Nurnberg coincidentally launched their own range of push-along 000-style toys to a gauge of 1:180 at around the same time. But it was a rival toy manufacturer in that same city – a centre of German toy-making for more than a century and perhaps better known in the UK as

RAPIDO IS BORN. . . Arnold's first N Gauge loco, the DB V200 diesel of 1960

Nuremberg – that we have to thank for becoming the first to marry 000 model trains and electrically-powered motors on 9mm track as a commercial venture.

Founded as far back as 1906, the family firm of K Arnold and Co of Nurnberg began by producing tinplate toys and related items including model ships and doll's house accessories for the German market.

Looking to diversify into other product lines in the late 1950s, Arnold was well aware of the increasing popularity of H0/00 electric trains and the company had watched local rival Trix's success with their push-along 000 models with enviable interest. While Arnold had not shown a close interest in model railways before, a decision was made to investigate the possibilities of putting electric motors inside 000-sized bodyshells and the result in 1960 was Rapido 200, with models at a scale of approximately 1:200 and a track width of 8mm.

The first locomotive, it has to be said, was a rather crude version of a V200 diesel loco of the Deutsche Bundesbahn rail network, which came with a set of three express coaches, and more items of rolling stock followed in the next few months.

The Arnold company's engineers clearly weren't happy with the original concept, however, because the range was re-worked and re-launched in 1962 as Arnold Rapido with a scale of 1:160 and track to the previous 000 standard of 9mm.

Subsequent products released under the Rapido banner were better designed and tooled and both locos and rolling stock – initially based almost exclusively on home-grown DB prototypes – were more accurate 2mm scale models. The first coupling mechanism was also a somewhat rudimentary affair, but within a couple of years, Arnold improved the design to create the Rapido coupling, compatible variants of which are used almost universally on most British and European proprietary N Gauge models today.

Arnold and rival German manufacturers were also instrumental in developing the term "N Gauge" for their products from around 1964 onwards. As we have seen, early 2mm modellers in the UK in the 1950s first adopted the term 000 (Treble-Oh) in a logical progression as the 00 track dimensions were halved again.

But this did not find favour elsewhere in the world, and there quickly became common agreement that 2mm to the foot models should be designated as N Gauge, with the letter standing for 9mm – the track width – as the world "nine" begins with the letter N in most major languages.

The launch of Rapido came as a jolt to both Lone Star and Trix. The two companies had been quietly developing their own electrified versions of their push-along trains and these were first marketed in their home countries before the end of 1960 – the Trix system of Continental-outline stock becoming known as Minitrix Electric and Lone Star's system re-launched as Treble-O-Lectric.

The latter ran on newly-designed track with the gauge modified to 9mm in common with both Minitrix and Rapido. None of the original Lone Star locos could run on the new track but some of the coaches and wagons were adapted with new chassis.

The new Lone Star electric 000 range was announced in the March 1960 issue of *Railway Modeller* and comprised two BR diesel locomotives – a Baby Deltic and a Class 24 – plus carriages, wagons, a station, bridges, other scenic items and, as mentioned above, a new range of trackwork. With sales in the US in mind, the North American "Transcontinental" diesel was retained in various liveries plus a US Baldwin steam loco and various items of US rolling stock.

The basic rubber-band drive mechanisms of the locos and the chunky appearance of the diecast rolling stock failed to impress many commentators

50 YEARS ON . . . Graham Farish's late 2008 diesel release, the Class 42 WR diesel hydraulic Warship of 1958, was of similar proportions to the German DB V200

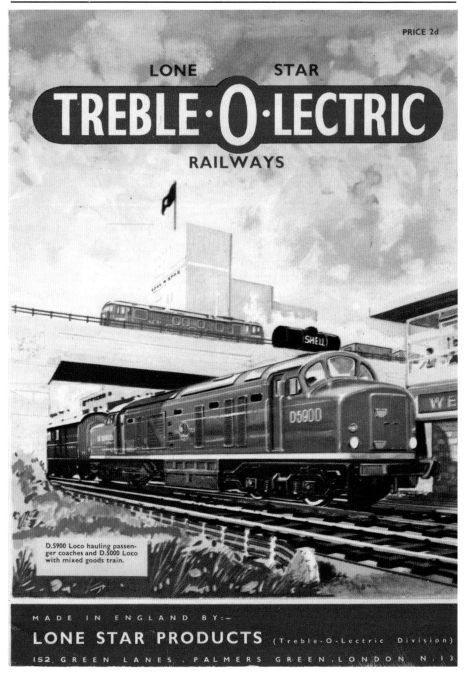

GO-GO-GO. . . Contemporary critics were scathing about the lack of speed control offered by Treble-O-Lectric's crude drive mechanisms and reliability problems

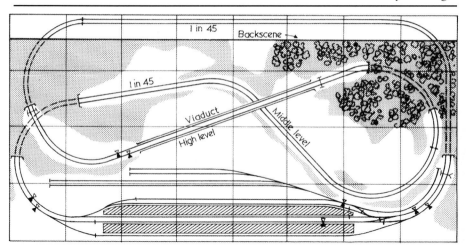

A NEW DIMENSION . . . The first layout plan to be designed for Lone Star's 000

at the time. But the new system found immediate support from the *Railway Modeller*'s then editor, Cyril Freezer, who pointed out that the advent of Lone Star's Treble-O-Lectric system meant that it was now possible for modellers to "contemplate a layout where really long trains run through sections of miniature countryside".

Indeed, he celebrated Lone Star's launch by publishing what is probably the first-ever track plan devised specifically with N Gauge in mind – under the prophetic heading of "000 – A New Dimension".

It was a false dawn, however. Treble-O-Lectric's somewhat crude appearance and basic drive mechanisms may have sufficed as a table-top toy system, but they were shunned by serious modellers. One contemporary reviewer – in an archived article spotted on the Internet – was particularly damning of the rubber-band drive system, which made it impossible for locos to "crawl". Indeed, he said: "There seems to be three speeds – Stop, Go-go-go and Fly-off-the-track."

Reliability problems also plagued the range, and by the mid-1960s, Lone Star had sadly fallen by the wayside, bringing an abrupt end – for a couple of years at least – to commercial British outline modelling in 2mm scale, as well as the effective death of the 000 model designation.

But Arnold and Minitrix were going from strength to strength on the Continent, and soon N Gauge fans in the UK were pondering the possibilities of scratchbuilding British locomotives utilising the German manufacturers' motors and chassis.

These ideas were given a boost in 1964 when Peco (the Devon-based Pritchard Patent Product Co) began producing trackwork and points in 9mm gauge to match their 00 products, followed by N Gauge wagon kits and a locomotive body kit to produce an ex-LMS Fairburn 2-6-4 tank which fitted on to an Arnold chassis. This was the first British outline loco in "true" N Scale and with its launch, British N Gauge could be said to have been born. It wasn't long before Peco were also offering a range of ready-to-run goods wagons that were the equal of their 00 products.

With the development of N Gauge in the UK set for take-off, we must take a pause at this point to return to the thorny problem of loading gauge differences which had bedevilled the early growth of H0/00 many years before to explain why N Gauge can mean different things in different areas of modelling.

While the 9mm track width adopted by both Lone Star and Arnold quickly became the universally-recognised N Gauge standard, the European adoption of 1:160 scale (1.91mm to the foot, to be exact) could only be accurately applied to models of European (and North American) prototypes because of their larger dimensions.

Pioneering UK modellers soon realised that the differences between Britain's loading gauge and the larger European loading gauge meant that British outline models would have to be proportionately bigger to run on scale-width 9mm track. Also, at least where steam locomotives were concerned, the bodies would have to be wider and taller to fit Continental-style chassis and motors.

So Peco – as the only British-outline N Gauge manufacturer at that time – decided that the compromise promoted by Henry Greenly for H0/00 in the 1920s should apply in the same way to British N Gauge – with the adoption of a new scale ratio of 1:148 (or 2.06mm to the foot). This gives a prototype track gauge equivalent of 4ft 4.5in – which may not be very accurate but actually compares favourably with British 00, which has a prototype track equivalent of only 4ft 1.5in.

The formation in 1967 of the N Gauge Society helped to set the Peco dimensions in stone, as it were, and when Graham Farish and Hornby Minitrix launched their N Gauge products in the early 1970s they followed suit. Since then all commercial British N Gauge products have followed the same scale.

Unsurprisingly, the purists of the 2mm Association did not agree, and they have continued to maintain British-outline modelling to a more accurate scale for 9mm track of 1:152.

To the newcomer to N Gauge modelling, it is hoped that this short history of the development of the scale has not proved too confusing to follow. Rest assured that if you want to model in British outline, just follow British outline practice. Likewise if you want to build a European, North American or Japanese layout (see Chapter 10), stick to those respective proprietary networks and you won't go wrong.

3 N Gauge Today

WHILE it is the intention of *N Gauge Modelling: An Introductory Guide* to give readers an overview of the complete N Gauge scene today, it is in recreating in miniature the British railway network of the past 60 years or so that the next chapters will focus.

Later in this book (Chapter 10), we'll take a closer look at modelling in European, North American and Japanese outline, but most would-be N Gauge modellers picking up this book will have a British layout idea in mind so that's where we'll make a start. Much of the following basic information regarding baseboards, tracklaying, electrics and even scenic construction apply to all layouts in all settings, but it is the boom in British outline N Gauge in the last decade or so that demands a closer look and to which *N Gauge Modelling: An Introductory Guide* is dedicated.

And what a choice is now available to the newcomer to the hobby and scale! The 2008 Bachmann-Graham Farish catalogue advertised no less than 435 items of rolling stock, including 44 steam locos and 75 diesels/electrics – including multiple units – plus 130 coaches and parcels vehicles from the 1930s through to the present day and 186 items of goods rolling stock covering almost every style and era of the same period.

At the same time, many other items produced by Graham Farish since the Bachmann takeover but absent from the 2008 catalogue remained in stock at model shops and mail order outlets around the country.

Dapol's range is growing by the month and also covers items from the last 75 years or so of the British scene, from 1930s GWR autocoaches to Virgin Voyagers and from pre-war private-owner coal wagons to modern-day cross-Continent Ferry Wagons and Freightliners. And don't forget the specialist manufacturers of N Gauge steam and diesel locos such as Ixion, CJM and Union Mills. In the next chapter, we'll take a closer look at layout styles and possible locations in the home, and also provide an overview on the wide choice of settings, in terms of era, which are available. But before that it might be helpful to newcomers to the hobby to bring the historical story up to date by documenting – albeit briefly – the development of N Gauge since those pioneering days in the early 1970s.

This is not just an academic exercise. Many N Gauge modellers first poke a toe into the 2mm water, as it were, by purchasing second-hand models from model shops, classified adverts, car boot sales and Internet sites like eBay, and this can prove a relatively inexpensive way to kick-start a layout. Many thousands of N Gauge locos and items of rolling stock have been produced for the UK scene over the past 40 years, and not just from the long-established market leaders, Graham Farish and Peco. Hornby Minitrix and Lima were also producing substantial quantities of British N Gauge items in the 1970s and 1980s.

Indeed, there is undoubtedly a thriving second-hand trade in 2mm scale items, particularly on eBay where on any given day you can find upwards of 3,000 N Gauge lots up for grabs – from entire layouts through locos and rolling stock old and new to single items of scenic accessory.

The Graham Farish company actually started back in 1919 as pioneers of another industry entirely – they specialised in the manufacture of wireless radios and wireless components, later moving on to other domestic appliances including heaters.

Looking to diversify after the Second World War, Farish spotted an opening in the model train market and launched a range of 00 flexible track – and then a range of 00 locomotives and rolling stock to run on it. The company thrived as a specialist 00 producer throughout the 1950s and 1960s as a rival to Peco but the company's fortunes really took off when they decided to move into the new N Gauge market in 1969.

Having seen how 2mm scale was gaining popularity in Europe and the US from the likes of Arnold and Fleischmann, it was clear that there was an opening for a serious manufacturer of British outline N Gauge items. Farish continued to manufacture 00 items into the 1980s but such was the success of their 2mm "Masterpieces in Miniature" range that they began to concentrate all new development in the scale from about 1972 onwards.

As with their 00 beginnings, the first items produced were flexible track with live-frog points, followed by more than a dozen different types of goods wagons. In 1971, a GWR 0-6-0 94XX pannier tank became the first locomotive in the range, quickly followed by an LNER J69 Holden tank in three liveries.

A GWR 4-6-0 Hall and three versions of Bulleid 4-6-2 Pacifics, plus suburban and mainline 57ft pre-nationalisation carriages in both BR and Big Four liveries

BLUE STAR: GWR 6021 King Richard II in BR's short-lived 1950s express blue would grace any mainline layout based on "God's Wonderful Railway" (Graham Farish)

and a greatly expanded range of goods wagons completed the offerings in the first few years of N Gauge production.

The Graham Farish range then developed extensively throughout the 1980s and 1990s to encompass an almost comprehensive range of steam and diesel locomotives, diesel railcars, HST sets, 25kv electrics, Mark 1, 2, 3 and 4 carriages and more than 200 different varieties of goods and parcels stock.

But Graham Farish was not the first firm to take up the Lone Star mantle and launch a British outline N gauge range. As we have seen, Minitrix was originally the name of a range of Lone Star-style push-along 000 trains launched in Germany in 1959 as an off-shoot of the German end of the Trix models business – a name with a complex and troubled history with both German and British antecedents dating back to 1930. Minitrix Electric was launched in Germany

DIESEL POWER: The Class 55 Deltics reigned supreme on the East Coast main line for 20 years from the end of steam to the electrification era   (Graham Farish)

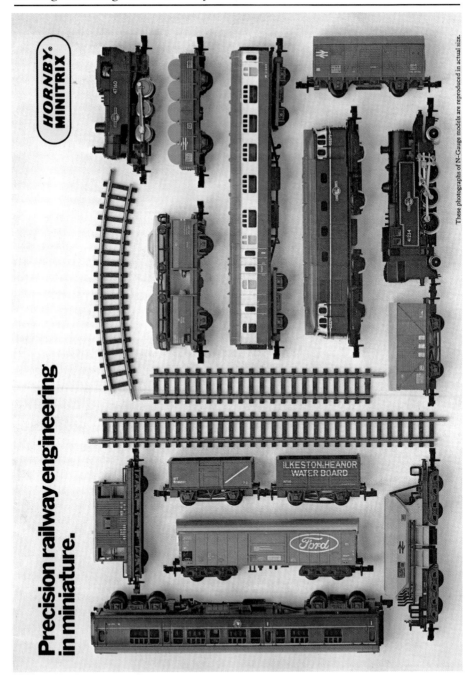

LIMITED RANGE . . . Hornby Minitrix products sold well for more than 10 years but modellers were frustrated by the lack of variety which restricted layout options

SUPERB STANIER . . . the LMS Corridor Second in early 1950s BR carmine and cream livery is a perfect match for a Farish Jubilee or Royal Scot (Graham Farish)

in 1960 and these early 000 models were imported into Britain and sold by the British Trix company, which following a series of complex amalgamations, re-organisations and takeovers had become part of the giant Courtaulds textile group. In 1964, a deal was made to assemble British outline locos based on the Class 26 diesel from German-supplied components, and space was provided at the Courtaulds-owned British Celanese factory in Wrexham, North Wales, for this purpose.

This venture was short-lived, however, because in 1967 Courtaulds decided to dispose of British Trix and following a few years of uncertainty, the British outline models were re-launched by the German Trix company from 1st January, 1973, with Liverpool-based Rovex Ltd, parent company of the Tri-ang Hornby

PERFECT PULLMAN . . . BR's blue and grey heyday in the 1970s saw the end of scheduled Pullman trains with a "reversed" version of the livery (Graham Farish)

COLLECTABLE . . .some Hornby Minitrix items are still in demand as they represent styles or liveries not available elsewhere, like this Ford car parts van.   (Pic: Adam Foy)

00 range, appointed as UK distributors – hence the new models were marketed as Hornby Minitrix.

Sales of Hornby Minitrix were considerable throughout the next 15 years, although modellers were disappointed that the range of N Gauge products available remained somewhat limited throughout the brand's heyday.

Indeed, just seven types of steam locomotives and three diesels, including the WR diesel-hydraulic Warship, were ever on offer, although livery variants meant that 21 different locos were modelled in all. Steam highlights included 7MT 70000 *Britannia*, 9F 92220 *Evening Star,* A4 60022 *Mallard* and A3 *Flying Scotsman* in both LNER and BR liveries.

Goods and passenger rolling stock was similarly restricted, with the latter amounting to variants of Mk 1 coaches in various BR liveries, and the former around a dozen different types of wagon, mostly in BR colours but with a selection of private-owner liveries as well. A few of the Minitrix wagons have become collectable due to their relative scarcity these days, particularly a car transporter wagon with four cars which was lifted directly from Minitrix's German offerings. To fill out the range, several other German wagons were sold as British – though slightly over-scale – disguised with new liveries.

Hornby Minitrix also offered a range of N Gauge track including electrically-operated points, plus a small number of scenic accessories, including signals and lineside builldings. Sadly, British Minitrix disappeared from the scene in the early 1990s following the expiry of Rovex Ltd's 15-year distribution deal. Euro Models & Toys took over from 1st January 1987 and the models continued to be marketed under the Mintrix banner, but supplies from the German factory became increasingly intermittent before drying up altogether.

In the mid-1990s Trix-Mangold, as the German parent company was now known, was experiencing financial troubles and in 1997 the entire Minitrix range was acquired by the Marklin company, who said at the outset that British Minitrix was unlikely to return for some time, if at all. More than a decade down the line, it seems that Hornby Mintrix is indeed history, which in many ways is a disappointment.

Their German parentage meant that the locos, in particular, were robust and well-engineered creations and they are still in demand by modellers today, as any glance at eBay will confirm. It is true that compromises had to be made to marry the German chassis to the British outline steam locos, particularly with the 2-10-0 9F, but many modellers in the 1970s and 1980s preferred them to the similar Farish products around at the time for their better pulling power and reliability. They regularly appear for sale on eBay and elsewhere, and some of the rarer items still command relatively high prices with collectors.

The Mk 1 coaches, which sold in their thousands, are also still regularly traded on the Internet and in model shops. Compared with the similar products on offer from Graham Farish today, the Minitrix Mk 1s are let down by the grossly over-scale window frames and inaccurate under-carriage details, but like all Minitrix products they were well-built and will last for years with careful handling. Many of the Minitrix goods wagons remain collectable as they represent styles and liveries not readily available elsewhere, such as the 1970s-style Ford car van.

Also entering the fray in the mid-1970s with British outline models was another Continental name with a complex history, Lima. The Lima company, of Vicenza in Italy, began manufacturing HO trains for the Continental market back in 1946, and moved into N Gauge, with Italian, French and Swiss diesel designs, in 1966.

As Lima's UK sales operation got under way, the British firm G & R Wrenn – by this time a subsidiary of Rovex following a takeover – was prompted to dip a toe in the N Gauge water and suggested a link-up with the Italian firm to produce some British outline stock. The result, somewhat oddly, was a decision to produce a Class 81 25kv electric locomotive on a Lima chassis as the first offering, with BR Mk 1 coaches in various liveries and a small range of good wagons including Freightliners.

These were marketed from mid-1968 as Wrenn N Gauge Micromodels, and the range slowly expanded to include a Class 31 diesel, a Class 04 0-4-0 diesel shunter and a Class 55 Deltic, all in green and blue BR liveries. At the same time, Wrenn began producing their own N Gauge track at their factory in Basildon, Essex.

Wrenn's link-up with Lima ended in 1977, after which the British outline stock was marketed by the parent company under the Lima name. Subsequent loco developments saw announcement of a first steam model, a roughly-proportioned 2-6-4 4MT Standard tank, an 0-6-0 94XX GWR pannier tank, 0-6-0 LNER J50 tank, GWR 4-6-0 *King George V* (and three named variants), 0-6-0 LMS 4F and the Class 52 Western diesel in four different liveries.

Confusingly, however, Lima's British outline sales lists at the time were padded out with several Continental and North American diesel designs with similarly-sequenced catalogue numbers and there were also some complete oddities listed in their range including the BR 4MT tank in Swedish (!) livery and also in GWR green.

Similar confusion ranged with their passenger and goods stock ranges with British, Continental and North American models all mixed up in the lists and some goods models purporting to be both British and Continental designs. The Mk 1 coaches were even listed in the colours of North America's Pennsylvania, Wabash, Santa Fe, New Haven and Baltimore & Ohio railroads! Not all the items listed in their catalogues ever made it to the production line, never mind the shops, so documenting the Lima N Gauge story is particularly difficult.

On the plus side for modellers at the time, Lima products were usually priced at up to 50% of the price of comparable Farish or Minitrix offerings, but on the down side, it has to be said that the quality of design and manufacture was markedly inferior, particularly with models of well-loved locos like the Deltic.

Loco bodies were recognisable copies of the originals but with major compromises in dimensions and construction to fit them on to Lima's Continental chassis. Passenger and goods rolling stock, likewise, were much cruder representations of originals than rival products.

Lima's British outline N Gauge venture was, like Minitrix, destined to be relatively short-lived. As Graham Farish's products improved and prospered, Lima's fortunes waned and by 1985 all British outline N Gauge production had ceased. There was briefly news of a possible revival of the name in 1991 when Arnold/Rivarossi, new owners of the Lima group, hinted at a British re-launch under the Lima MiniTrains banner, but nothing came of the proposals.

Lima's British outline N Gauge items also appear regularly in second-hand sales lists, though they are not as common as Hornby Minitrix and rarely attract as much demand. More than 20 years after the range's demise, it is difficult to recommend most of these products to the serious N Gauge modeller, although well cared-for items could provide the basis of a cheap starter layout.

The only other ready-to-run British-outline loco available in the 1970s

FINEST SCALE. . . the Peco LMS Jubilee – here represented in maroon by preserved example 5690 Leander – set new standards for British-outline N Gauge (Pic: Adam Foy)

and 1980s was the splendid LMS 4-6-0 Jubilee offered by Peco. This was manufactured for the Devon company by the Italian firm Rivarossi and most modellers of that era would agree that it was the finest N Gauge model available at that time. Indeed, to some observers, its Continental parentage helped it set a standard for RTR N Gauge in the UK which was not to be equalled, let alone surpassed, for many years to come.

Peco is now one of the most familiar names in Britain to railway modellers, especially in N Gauge, and, as we have seen, the company's pioneering efforts were pivotal in the development of British-outline 2mm scale modelling from the late 1960s onwards.

Peco was founded in 1945 as the trading name of the Pritchard Patent Product Co, a business set up by the late Stanley Pritchard to produce model railway items he had begun designing in his spare time. The first product was the Simplex model railway coupling for 00 modellers, and soon he was making 00 flexible track under the Pecoway banner plus components for hand-building track in that gauge.

In 1951, Peco acquired the *Railway Modeller* magazine from Ian Allan, a canny move as the publication not only advanced the hobby but also acted as a shop window for Peco products, which quickly developed into 00 white metal wagon kits and then ready-built wagons.

The first 2mm items to come from the Devon factory were Minilay track-making components, which were initially offered to scratchbuild modellers in

9.5mm gauge – the early 000 format. In 1961, Peco became official distributors of the Lone Star Treble-O-Lectric models and the Minilay track was adapted to 9mm to fit. A year later, they became the UK distributors for the Arnold range of Continental models, and the ready availability of Arnold steam and diesel chassis allowed Peco to launch a series of British outline body kits in 1965, including the 2-6-4 LMS Fairburn tank and Class 35 Hymek diesel-hydraulic.

In 1964, the new Streamline ready-built flexible track was launched and Peco began actively promoting the new scale, initially still under the 000 banner, despite Continental firms announcing that they would call the scale N Gauge from now on.

As with 00, the first rolling stock on offer was a series of white metal goods wagon kits, but the ready-made Wonderful Wagons – nowadays marketed in N Gauge as Quality Line – were launched in 1967. For a brief period, Minitrix Mk1 coaches were also marketed by Peco alongside the goods vehicles under the Wonderful Coaches banner.

In late 1968, a link-up with the Italian firm Rivarossi saw Peco marketing in the UK a range of N Gauge items intended for the North American market, and a year later, the Devon firm launched its 4-6-0 LMS Jubilee loco No 5713 *Renown*, which was made for it by Rivarossi.

Unusually for the UK N Gauge market, later variants of the Jubilee from 1973

WONDERFUL WAGONS . . . Now known under the generic name "Quality Line", Peco's N Gauge goods vehicle range runs to around 100 different models (Pic: Peco)

onwards were provided in plain livery without names and numbers to allow the purchaser to select from a series of alternate identities on transfers included with the loco. The transfers changed with later batches of locos, allowing for up to 16 different identities to be produced.

Frustratingly, however, the early models came only in LMS black, necessitating a repaint for anyone who wanted to run a Jubilee on a BR layout. In 1982, a maroon version appeared, still in LMS configuration, but a BR green variety later followed – although judging by the number of Peco Jubilees which come up for sale on the Internet and elsewhere, sales of this latter version must have been quite small.

Later variants also saw the introduction of plug-in double chimneys for those locos which carried them, and for experienced modellers there was even a conversion kit to turn the Jubilee into a rebuilt Patriot or Royal Scot, two sister LMS classes with broadly similar dimensions.

The Peco Jubilee disappeared from the company's catalogue after 1991, as Peco concentrated, in N Gauge at any rate, on their huge variety of wagons and scenic accessories, plus three kinds of track – Setrack and Code 55 and Code 80 flexible. The company is also a major manufacturer, of course, in 0, 00 and 009 – the narrow-gauge system which also uses 9mm track.

It was, nevertheless, something of a surprise when Peco announced a return

VEHICLE VARIETY. . . the Peco four-wheel wagon range covers the pre-war Big Four and private owner companies through BR's heyday to the modern scene (Pic: Peco)

WELCOME BACK . . . 15 years after the demise of the Jubilee, Peco returned to the RTR N Gauge loco scene in 2006 with the GWR Collett Goods 0-6-0   (Pic: Peco)

to the N Gauge ready-to-run market in the UK in 2006. The loco is the GWR 0-6-0 Collett Goods which comes DCC-ready – and it was widely welcomed as filling in a major gap in the GWR ready-to-run market in N.

While Hornby Minitrix, Lima and Peco concentrated on just a few N Gauge items, Graham Farish steadily extended their range throughout the 1980s and early 1990s until most eras were catered for, from the Big Four of the 1930s through to post-privatisation companies like Virgin and GNER.

In the summer of 2000, word reached the modelling fraternity that Graham Farish, a family-owned and wholly British operation since its founding, was about to be sold to the American giant Bachmann Industries Europe Ltd, which had been making steady inroads into the British 00 market since 1989 and now rivalled Hornby in the larger scale.

The takeover meant the closure of Farish's little factory in Poole, Dorset, and relocation to Bachman's Leicestershire HQ, with the actual manufacture of models being out-sourced to China. There was much initial trepidation among N Gauge modellers about this move, and certainly in the early days of the takeover, many Farish items disappeared from the shops as old stocks were run down and delays developed in re-tooling and re-design for the switch to China.

The first models emerged from the factories in the Far East in mid-2001 – a few wagons plus re-tooled HST sets in Midland Mainline and GNER colours and the Class 158 DMU in five different liveries. Further models re-joined the range in limited numbers over the next few months until Chinese production was in full swing.

The first years of this millennium saw the Graham Farish range expanding in an unprecedented scale with re-tooled models whose quality of manufacture and finish are undoubtedly superior to the old Farish products and, indeed, bear comparison with anything Bachmann produces in 00 outline. On takeover, Bachmann announced that all new Farish locos and multiple units would feature the Bachmann 5-pole skew-wound motor, which provides greatly-improved traction and reliability compared with the old Poole products.

There have been several welcome additions to the old Farish range too, starting with a completely new steam model, the LNER V2, and the much-welcomed Peak class diesels, Stanier Jubilees and – bringing the railway story bang up to date, Class 220/221 Virgin Voyagers and Class 60 and 66 diesels. N Gauge modellers can hopefully look forward to even more variety to come as Bachmann recently pledged that the company's aim was for their entire British outline 00 range to be replicated in the smaller scale eventually.

Just as Farish had Hornby Minitrix and Lima as rivals in the 1970s and 1980s, today sees another major rival to the long-established "Masterpieces in Miniature". This is Dapol, another former 00 kit maufacturer which has been re-born in the new century as a producer of superb British ready-to-run N Gauge models.

Dapol's entry into the N Gauge market came in a modest way towards the end of 2003 when the North Wales-based company announced the launch of B-set GWR coaches in pre-war and BR maroon liveries, and two GWR siphon bogie

21st CENTURY RAILS . . . The Cross-Country Virgin Voyagers introduced following privatisation are already history since franchise changes in 2007 (Graham Farish)

ELECTRO-FYING . . . Dapol's Class 73 Electro-Diesel has been released in several liveries including GB Railfreight (Photo supplied and reproduced by permission of Dapol Ltd)

goods vans, which filled valuable gaps in the Farish range. Many modellers assumed initially that 2mm rolling stock was the limit of Dapol's ambitions, but any such thoughts were turned on their head a few months later with the announcement of a GWR 14XX 0-4-2 tank loco and matching auto-coach.

They followed up in 2005 with a GWR Prairie 45XX 2-6-2T and then a Class 73 Electro-Diesel, another model previously unavailable in RTR form in 2mm, and one much welcomed by modellers who favoured a Southern Region locale. Over the next 12 months or so this was released in at least eight different liveries and identities, from BR blue through Intercity, Pullman, EWS and South West Trains colours.

The 73 was followed in 2005 by the Class 66, again in several different liveries and identities, and then the Class 220/221 Virgin Voyager made its debut in late 2006. It is a pity, in some respects, that the latter two models have also been duplicated in the Graham Farish range, but the wealth of different models available, particularly of the 66s, means that modellers of the present-day scene have never had it so good. A particularly welcome feature of Dapol's production policy is the issue of locos in batches of different numbers to allow a sizeable stud of the same model to be built up without recourse to repaints and renumbering.

In 2008, they launched the Class 35 Hymek diesel-hydraulic and then there was more duplication as both companies announced production of the BR Standard 9F, a loco previously available in N Gauge from Hornby Minitrix. Graham Farish promised three variants, including 92220 *Evening Star*, the last steam locomotive to be built by British Railways in 1960. Dapol's 2008 catalogue listed no less than eight different 9Fs with both single and double chimney variants and two different tenders. Later in the year, they announced production of *Evening Star* also.

Alongside their locos, Dapol have also been steadily increasing their

WESTERN WORKHORSE . . . Dapol's 2008 release of the Class 35 Hymek filled another gap for WR modellers (Photo supplied and reproduced by permission of Dapol Ltd)

impressive range of passenger and goods vehicles with both Big Four and modern varities, many of which have not been available in 2mm previously.

Finally, mention should be made here of a handful of small manufacturers who make "bespoke" models – often at premium prices! The newest of these is Australian-based Ixion Models, who launched a magnificent GWR Manor loco in September 2008. Union Mills, a small Isle of Man-based company, specialises in the production of pre-nationalisation steam goods locos, while CJM, Ian Stoate and Millfield Models offer finely detailed versions of diesel and electric locos.

As mentioned in Chapter 2, all RTR British-outline models from whatever manufacturer are fitted with the Arnold Rapido-style auto-coupling so there are no compatibility problems when running trains made up of vehicles from various sources.

While being horrendously over-scale and non-prototypical, the N Gauge coupling is reliable and easy to operate and has the advantage over the Hornby and Bachmann-style RTR 00 coupling of permitting a coach or wagon to be extricated easily from a rake by hand with one simple upward movement.

MAGNIFICENT MANOR . . . The new GWR 4-6-0 from Australian firm Ixion is a superb model in BR and GWR guise (Photo by Lindsay O'Reilly/Ixion Model Railways Ltd)

4 When and Where

THE wide variety of products now on offer in both 00 and N Gauge recently prompted Bachmann and other manufacturers to adopt a format of railway "eras" in which to categorise their products as an aid to modellers. It has to be said that this system has not been universally welcomed by hobbyists, and the letters pages of the railway modelling magazines and Internet forums initially carried complaints and criticisms of the "eras" selected.

But much of the carping seems of a nit-picking nature and Bachmann, in particular, are to be commended for their attempt to simplify around 200 years of railway history. And newcomers to the hobby in particular will no doubt find the branding of items in the Bachmann catalogues helpful when considering a possible subject for a layout.

Bachmann have split that history into nine clearly-defined eras, starting with the birth of railways, which it is assumed they identify as being Cornishman Richard Trevithick's creation of the steam-operated Penydarren tramroad near Merthyr Tydfil in South Wales in 1804. They are as follows:

1: 1804-1875 – the "Pioneering" days
2: 1875-1922 – Pre-Grouping
3: 1923-1947 – The Big Four of the LMS, LNER, GWR and SR.
4: 1948-1956 – British Railways early emblem (lion-on-wheel logo)
5: 1957-1966 – British Railways later emblem ("shirt-button" logo)
6: 1967-1971 – BR Blue pre-TOPS (ie. D-prefix numbering)
7: 1971-1982 – BR Blue TOPS (ie. Class numbering)
8: 1982-1994 – BR Sectorisation
9: 1995-onwards – Post-Privatisation

Eras 1 and 2 are very much specialist subjects in any gauge, and only the

QUIRKY Q1 ... Bulleid's stripped-down wartime "Austerity" locos were Southern freight stalwarts into the 1960s   (Photo supplied and reproduced by permission of Dapol Ltd)

most determined and skilled scratchbuild modellers would attempt an N Gauge layout in either.

The Big Four era between the two world wars is reasonably well catered for with RTR products from Bachmann-Graham Farish and selected models from Dapol. For the LMS, Stanier 8Fs and Black Fives, Crab 2-6-0s, Fowler 4Fs, Compound 4-4-0s, Duchess Pacifics and Jubilees have all been available, plus the recently released Stanier coaches. From Dapol comes the Ivatt 2-6-2 2MT tank. For the LNER, A3s, A4s and V2s have been offered plus Gresley teak coaches from both GF and Dapol, plus the recent B17 "Footballers" from Dapol. Second-hand A3s and A4s can be found from Hornby Minitrix.

For the GWR, there are Halls, Castles, Kings, Pannier Tanks, Prairie tanks and diesel railcars from Graham Farish, 45XX tanks from Dapol plus the new Collett 0-6-0 tender Goods from Peco and a new Manor from Ixion/Dapol. GW coaching stock is available from Farish and Dapol and the latter also offers the 14XX tank loco which can run with the appropriate coach in auto-trailer formation.

For the Southern Railway, the choice is more limited but there have been

WOODEN WONDERS ... Gresley's 1930s teak coaches look just right behind an LNER "Footballer", A3 or V2 (Photo supplied and reproduced by permission of Dapol Ltd)

LAST OF THE LINE . . . BR's final steam locomotive Evening Star, built in 1960, is one of Dapol's latest offerings (Photo supplied and reproduced by permission of Dapol Ltd)

Battle of Britain, West Country and Merchant Navy Pacifics in original Spam Can form plus Dapol's M7 tank, while the latter also recently issued Bulleid's quirky Q1 in SR livery.

As far as goods stock is concerned, there are dozens of varieties of Big Four and private owner wagons currently available from Graham Farish, Peco and Dapol, with many others to be found second-hand from Hornby Minitrix and Lima.

Once we get to the post-1948 Nationalisation era, the choice for layouts set in most areas of Britain is reasonably comprehensive. For most modellers planning a BR steam layout, Eras 4 and 5 can be effectively the same thing – certainly in a layout set in the period 1958-64 – as locos in BR black, Brunswick Green and LMS maroon ran with both versions of the original BR tender logo in the late 1950s and early 1960s with the switch from lion-on-wheel to "shirt-button" styles dependent on the vagaries of shed policies, overhauls and repaints.

All the steam locos mentioned above from the "Big Four" era are also available in one or both BR tender/tank logos and various guises – including rebuilt Bulleid Pacifics – while the post-nationalisation Standard Classes are represented by 4MT and 3MT tanks from Graham Farish, Britannia Pacifics from Hornby Minitrix and the Riddles 9F 2-10-0s from three different sources – new from Dapol and Farish and second-hand from Hornby Minitrix. The Ivatt BR 2-6-0 mixed traffic loco can also be found in both green and black liveries from the latter.

Mention should also be made here of the Isle of Man-based Union Mills company, a cottage industry producing various small goods locos based on LNER, LMS and Southern designs in both pre-and post-nationalisation guises.

In coaching stock, the carmine and cream ("blood and custard") livery adopted at the dawn of nationalisation for most regions gave way to maroon in the mid-1950s but you can mix and match rakes of each livery or even a mixture of liveries with equanimity, and if you are modelling WR or SR locations you have the choice of sticking to BR's original chocolate-and-cream and Southern green regional identities respectively or mixing with other liveries.

Era 5 also encompasses diesels in their original green liveries and Graham Farish has produced Classes 04, 08, 20, 25, 31, 33, 37, 40, 42, 44, 45, 46, 47 and 55 in this colour both before and since the Bachmann takeover. Classes 27 and 42 can also be found in green from Hornby Minitrix.

There are similar overlaps between the later diesel eras. Era 6, for instance, encompasses D-numbered blue diesels – in all the above-mentioned classes – but you can also mix in yet-to-be-repainted green versions and at least until mid-1968 – in parts of the London Midland region at least – you can even add certain steam classes like Black Fives, 8Fs and some Standard designs which survived until the very end of steam on BR on 11th August that year. There are even well-documented examples of steam locos pulling rakes of blue-and-white coaches on football and rugby specials and enthusiasts' excursions into the summer of 1968.

Eras 6 and 7 can be largely inter-changeable, too, because you only have to set your layout in, say 1971, to have both pre and post-TOPS diesels and electrics running together – and also added to the mix is the Class 50 from Graham Farish in its WR guise. Likewise the early 1980s would see a mix of TOPS blue and Sectorisation liveries, and the mid-1990s could see a mix of Sector liveries and the colourful first post-Privatisation designs.

Diesel-lovers are now particularly well catered-for in N Gauge as almost all BR classes in service from the early 1960s to the present day are currently available or can be found second-hand in a variety of liveries. Models of the Brush Class 47, for example, can be found in two-tone BR green, all-over BR

PERFECT PEAK . . . One of the first Peak class diesels, D8 Penyghent, in its 1970s blue guise post-TOPS re-classification as Class 44 No 44 008   (Graham Farish)

THUNDERBIRDS ARE GO . . . The Brush 47/57 looks great in many liveries, but the Virgin Thunderbird look is arguably the most attractive of them all (Graham Farish)

blue, blue with large double-arrow logo, original InterCity livery, Swallow livery, Scotrail, freight Sectorisation, Rail Express, RES, First Great Western, Virgin, EWS, Freightliner, Fragonset and DRS blue, to name only some. And that's not to mention the Class 57 variants in Virgin Thunderbird, Porterbrook, Direct Rail Services, First Great Western and Freightliner colours. Some livery variations have not been produced since the Bachmann takeover but most of these can readily be found in the second-hand market.

Regarding the modern-day scene, there has been an unfortunate element of duplication in recent years with both Graham Farish and Dapol producing the Class 66 diesel in various liveries and, more recently, the Class 220/221 Virgin Voyager in several different named guises.

Of course, the beauty of railway modelling, even if you choose a British outline subject, is that you don't have to stick to any strict era or location. You can opt for a totally fictitious scheme in which you can run any locomotives – steam and/or diesel – and rolling stock that takes your fancy.

By selecting a rural location and keeping scenic elements to a bare minimum, it is even possible to construct a layout which you could convincingly set in inter-changeable eras from the pre-war Big Four period to the present-day.

The wild northern heights of the Settle & Carlisle, for instance, have changed hardly at all in the last 70 years or so, except for minor elements like signalling and removal of sidings. Assuming you have the requisite stock available, you could run an S&C layout in LMS days in ome session and then switch over to, say, the post-privatisation 1990s next time.

Let's now assume you have selected an era or fictitious subject you wish to model. Before we go any further with some detailed planning of your layout,

FREIGHT POWER . . . The Class 60 is one of GF's newest models and comes in three guises, including 60084 Cross Fell in Transrail triple grey livery (Graham Farish)

the thorny question of where to put it must be faced. Basically, there are five possible locations in and around the home to place a model railway – a spare room, the garage, the loft, the cellar (in older houses) or in a garden shed.

Each location has its advantages and disadvantages and it is not the intention of this book to go into too much detail about this topic. All would-be modellers will know what space is available and will have to decide for themselves on the best position for their particular project, but a short summary of the pros and cons of each may be helpful.

A spare room is, without a doubt, the optimum location for any railway layout. Assuming that it is truly spare – ie. not needed for any other household purpose – then the design and extent of your layout need only by determined by your efforts, your skills and your budget. Even allowing for almost unlimited space, it is important not to get carried away, particularly if you are a beginner. Other determining factors that come into play include operating flexibility. Many a modeller, in whatever scale, has designed and constructed a "dream" layout that has turned into a nightmare because it needed more than one person to operate satisfactorily.

A spare room that has to double up as an occasional bedroom is slightly less than ideal because compromises may have to be agreed in terms of folding away to accommodate visitors or removing and storing whole sections. This need not be a problem if such flexibility is built into the original design and construction.

Talking of "spare" rooms, avoid the idea of building a layout in a conservatory-style house extension built to catch the sun. Large expanses of glass can produce high temperatures which can damage both models and the layouts themselves.

The next most popular location for a layout is a domestic garage. Some dedicated modellers opt to leave the car outside at all times to utilise the full space available – and the average garage can certainly accommodate a big N Gauge layout! Alternatively, a fold-down layout or one that can be quickly dismantled for storage is the best bet, although dampness can be a major problem – particularly if a rain-soaked car is regularly parked in the garage alongside a layout to dry out. There is also a danger of introducing air-borne particles of dirt from outside which can settle on your layout and play havoc with loco mechanisms and electrical connections.

Extremes of temperature can also cause problems in the third most popular household location – a loft or attic. House lofts can provide more useable space than any other part of the home but before building a layout there you must ensure that it is dry (no leaks whatsoever) and – paradoxically – it must be both well-ventilated for hot spells and insulated against the cold. Some form of heating will almost certainly be needed if you plan to use the loft in the depths of winter.

One other factor to bear in mind is ease of access. A rickety ladder on the landing beneath a narrow opening in the ceiling will not provide the most convenient access to your layout and you must remember that every part of the baseboard will have to go through the opening, which will probably rule out any advance construction work in more comfortable surroundings.

Location No 4 in terms of popularity is a garden shed. Assuming you have garden space available, this can be the best spot for a layout and the smaller size of N Gauge is particularly suited to this idea. Layout-sized timber sheds are inexpensive and can be purchased from any DIY superstore in kit form. They usually require no planning permission (but do check first!) and anyone who can build a model railway should be able to erect one (with help) in a weekend.

For most sheds with basic timber walls and floor, insulation is vital, including a damp-proof base, and don't forget you will need to provide a mains power supply for the layout itself, for lighting, and, of course heating. Please note also that these days, thanks to some very sensible health and safety legislation, there are very strict Institution of Electrical Engineers (IEE) regulations which lay down rules about running mains electricity to an outbuilding.

It is no longer permissible to add a permanent connection by means of a flexible cable and even a temporary lead must be fed though a residual current device (RCD) which is a quick-acting safety socket. Professional advice and, preferably, professional installation is recommended. When considering a shed for your layout don't overlook the question of security. It might be wise to store valuable locomotives and rolling stock in the house when out of use.

Finally, if you live in an older house with a basement or cellar, this can also

NO ROOM FOR A LAYOUT? . . . This is Ashcombe, a diorama-style GWR branchline layout exhibited by John Spence at the September 2008 Warwickshire N Gauge show. It measures just 4ft x 2ft, plus two 1ft boards on each side to take the track round to the fiddle-yard behind the backscene. These are hinged and fold up for storage (HF)

be a good place to build a layout. As with a loft, you'll probably have more space than you'll actually need or can make use of, but once again you'll have to ensure that the entire space is dry and insulated before you can consider using it to play trains.

Of course, N Gauge's small size means that there are other possible household locations for a layout with a little ingenuity. An L-shaped branchline terminus could easily be accommodated on a shelf less than a foot (30cm) wide and with each arm only 3-4ft (0.9-1.2 m) long it would fit in the corner of even the smallest room. It is even possible – with a lift-out section for the door – to build a continuous run around a room on a shelf of similar dimensions, perhaps utilising the rear of cupboards or wardrobnes as "tunnel" sections.

It is also possible to construct small N Gauge layouts in alcoves under stairs, on landings, on top of bookshelves or cupboards, mounted on ironing boards or even built into coffee tables in the lounge. At a recent N Gauge exhibition, there was a fascinating display of layouts in unlikely settings that got smaller and smaller, culminating in a continuous run built into a briefcase!

5 Laying It Out

THE space available to you when planning a layout will, of course, have an overbearing influence on the next choice to be made – the actual configuration of layout to be constructed. There are essentially four basic configurations to be considered – end-to-end, continuous loop, out and back, or station-to-fiddle yard – although combinations of two or more elements can widen the options even further.

For instance, you can combine a branch-line terminus with a continuous run, or, where space permits, an end-to-end can be turned into a "dumb-bell" or "dog-bone" layout in which reversing loops at either end can be used to turn trains back so that they pass through the layout in both directions. The loops can also be multi-tracked to provide storage space.

Beginners would be advised to stick to one basic configuration, however, and a combination of personal choice and the space available will be the defining factors. Whether you want to model a branch-line terminus, a busy main-line station a rural cross-country line or a busy industrial location, you will be limited in scope by your chosen location in the home.

No two layouts are identical and it is impossible to be dogmatic and set hard-and-fast rules here about minimum dimensions for any particular style, but broadly speaking the smallest space for a branch-line terminus-to-fiddle yard plan in N Gauge would be the dimensions of the corner shelf design mentioned in the previous chapter – say 3-4ft in length and 9-12in wide for each of the two arms.

A continuous loop can be built in a briefcase, but the smallest practical dimensions to allow for sidings and some operational flexibility would be 4ft x 2ft (1.2m x 0.6m) – or slightly bigger if you want a double-track loop. The loop configuration can be a simple table-top style oval as modelled on the ready-made Magnum layout formerly produced by Graham Farish, or a through station or countryside line linked at both ends to a fiddle yard. Either of these configurations can be doubled in length by turning the run through a looped figure-of-eight formation, although construction of the latter will of necessity be

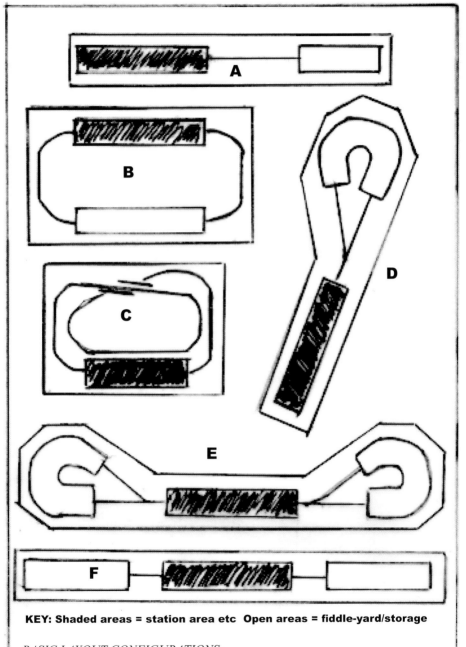

KEY: Shaded areas = station area etc   Open areas = fiddle-yard/storage

BASIC LAYOUT CONFIGURATIONS:
A: Station to fiddle-yard, B: Continuous loop, C: Figure-of-eight loop,
D: Out and back, E: "Dumb-bell" End-to-End, F: Basic End-to-End

UP AND DOWN . . . Littlewood featured two steep gradients linking the diesel depot (top right of picture) to the upper and lower running lines for transfer of locomotives

more complex because of the need to introduce gradients and different levels of track – two elements which would benefit by a longer baseboard than 4ft x 2ft.

An out-and-back layout in which trains leave a location, perhaps to join a continuous run, before being permitted to return to the point of departure can also be built in that same space of 4ft x 2ft by folding lines over each other and introducing gradients, but if you want to keep trains on one level, you'll probably need twice that amount of space.

End-to-end runs from fiddle-yard to fiddle-yard will need a minimum track storage length of around 3ft (1m) at either end if trains are kept to a maximum of loco plus three coaches, plus whatever length the visible central section of the layout is intended to be, and a minimum width of 9-12in (23-30cm), although clever designs can fold the run back on itself to give overall layout dimensions which are considerably more compact.

Station-to-station end-to-ends will need probably double those dimensions for a satisfactory layout, although such designs are not really suited to one-man operation as they are effectively two layouts joined by a running line.

You can squeeze more layout into a given space by introducing gradients so that one track can pass over another, but these have their own problems – particularly for the beginner. Rail gradients in real life are normally expressed by a ratio in which a given number of units of length is needed to gain one unit of height. In other words, a 1 in 100 gradient means that the track must travel for 100 yards/metres in distance to achieve a height gain of one yard/metre.

You need around 30-33mm of height to achieve a simple rail crossover in N Gauge, measured by the distance from the bottom rail's height to the underside of a bridge. But when you take into account the trackbed needed to support the top rails, the vertical distance is more like 40mm. In theory, you could install such a cross-over with a 1 in 30 gradient in just under four feet (4.9 metres) of track distance.

In the real world, an incline of 1 in 30 is unknown in the UK on standard gauge lines and anything under 1 in 50 is regarded as excessively steep The notorious Dainton Bank on the Great Western main line in Devon at 1 in 36 and the Lickey Incline south of Birmingham at around 1 in 37 are the most severe on the national network, and they are very much the exceptions that prove the rule where UK rail gradients are concerned. Even the 1 in 100 ruling gradient of the famous Long Drag on the Settle & Carlisle is a significant incline.

As well as looking very much un-protoypical, a 1 in 30 incline in N could also cause problems of stalling for your rolling stock, particularly with older steam locos, and 3-4 coaches or 10 four-wheeler wagons would be the maximum length of a train which would negotiate such an incline easily. A 1 in 50 incline – still regarded as very steep in railway terms – would need a run of around 75 inches (roughly 2 metres) to clear that 40mm crossover, while a 1 in 100 gradient would need a minimum of about 150 inches (4 metres). You could halve these dimensions however, if you have one track rising and the other track falling by the same elevation.

Gradients should also start and end with a gradual transformation back to level track, not a sudden switch of elevation as if the track was surmounting a wedge of cheese. If anything, this would add another 9-12in (23-30cm) to the length needed.One neat way to change the level of your track where space for your layout is at a premium is to introduce a spiral in a hidden section – and at least one commercial firm with regular adverts in the modelling press now offers these ready-made. This can be particularly useful with an end-to-end or terminus-to-fiddle yard formation but on a continuous run you'll need two such spirals – at either end of your layout – to allow trains to return to the base level.

Once you have settled on the dimensions of your layout, you can get down to detailed planning of the proposed track formation. Layout planning is almost a hobby in itself and there are few modellers who haven't doodled layout ideas on odd scraps of paper at idle moments – either realistic schemes or fantasy designs. If pushed, some modellers – this writer included – will admit that they can actually nod themselves off to sleep not by counting sheep or even railway trucks but by imagining that perfect layout and the train formations they would run on it.

There are a handful of basic rules which you should keep in mind at all times when drawing up a detailed track plan – if only to stop yourself getting carried away by trying to achieve the impossible! These can be summarised thus:

1. Your plan must fit the space available.
2. It must be practical to construct, maintain and operate.
3. It must provide ready accessibility to all areas of track at all times.
4. It must have curves and gradients within workable limits for the stock you intend to operate.
5. It must provide sufficient siding and/or storage accommodation for your stock.
6. It must provide sustainable operating interest.

Most of these points are self-explanatory although *N Gauge Modelling: An Introductory Guide* will be going into them all in more detail in the course of the following chapters. However, it is perhaps pertinent to single out No 3 for a little expansion here. Your layout must not to be too wide, or positioned, say, in a corner of a room, where you cannot easily reach by hand any part of the running track at any time.

The simple reason for this is that with the best will in the world you can never be 100% sure that at some stage during an operating session you won't suffer a loco stalling or a wagon de-railing or becoming uncoupled – and sod's law states that this will be in the most inaccessible area if such a spot exists. Realistically, the average adult's reach is no more than 3ft (1metre) from the edge of a baseboard, and this should be your ruling maximum.

Similarly, and for the same reason, all hidden sections of the track formation should also be fully accessible by leaving at least fist-sized openings in backscenes etc or removable top sections which can easily be built into your scenery and disguised. Don't think you can get away by squeezing fingers through a tunnel entrance or, worse still, poking through the opening with a ruler or pencil to extricate recalcitrant rolling stock. Not only will you risk damaging the vehicles, but you could also do serious damage to your carefully-constructed scenery!

For newcomers to the hobby, Peco offer some handy and inexpensive booklets, including a *Setrack Planbook, N Gauge Track Plans* and *60 Plans For Small Locations,* which are worthy of study. For more detailed planning, C.J. Freezer's *Model Railway Design Manual* (PSL) first published in 1996, is highly recommended for an exhaustive general overview of the subject. There are other general books available on railway modelling, which contain much

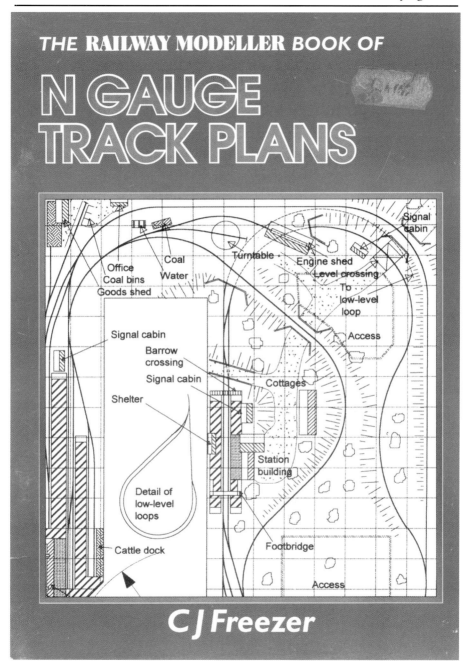

THE RAILWAY MODELLER BOOK OF

N GAUGE TRACK PLANS

Labels within diagram:
- Signal cabin
- Turntable
- Engine shed
- Level crossing
- To low-level loop
- Access
- Office
- Coal bins
- Goods shed
- Coal
- Water
- Signal cabin
- Barrow crossing
- Signal cabin
- Cottages
- Shelter
- Station building
- Detail of low-level loops
- Cattle dock
- Footbridge
- Access

CJ Freezer

GOOD ADVICE . . The Railway Modeller. Book of N Gauge Track Plans is just one of the inexpensive guides produced by Peco to help in planning of a 2mm layout valuable information on planning and usually include a few suggested plans, the most recent of which is Iain Rice's *Railway Modelling The Realistic Way* (Haynes) published in late 2007.

Don't forget, too, that the monthly modelling magazines often feature ideas for N Gauge track plans, while plans for 00 gauge can often be adopted or scaled down. Please note, however, that it is often a mistake to think you can simply reduce any 00 scale plan to quarter-size for N Gauge. In many cases the result can be a disappointment because features of track design compromises which work well in the larger scale such as point diagrams and sharp curves can seem unrealistic or even toy-like when reduced to 2mm.

These differences are accentuated by the fact that the viewing position remains the same above the layout in both gauges, but in N Gauge that viewpoint is effectively twice as high as in 00. Also, clearances between crossover tracks cannot be reduced by the same proportion as other elements, which is likely to cause major problems in re-engineering gradients.

Off-the-peg designs encompass both real and fantasy locations and the first-time modeller can copy a favoured plan wholesale or use it as a basis for an altered version. Layout plans can now also be found in CD-Rom form, although many are based on North American or European locations.

Finally, there are several commercial services available in which experienced modellers will design detailed track plans to particular specifications. Again, the newcomer is referred to adverts in the monthly modelling magazines.

Whatever type of layout you want, there are a couple of basic restrictions that you must take into account at the planning stage. The first is the minimum radius available for curved sections. As mentioned earlier, N Gauge stock will turn through 180 degrees in a baseboard width of as little as 20in (500mm), a radius of around 9in (230mm). But such severe curves are absolutely non-prototypical and even when placed in hidden sections, such curves can lead to derailments with troublesome stock at anything but the slowest speeds.

Curves of 12in will still bring trains round through 180 degrees in a width of 2ft (0.6m) without problems, although such curves should still be kept hidden as long trains of coaches or bogie wagons negotiating such sharp bends can look quite ridiculous.

The second restriction on planning will be your optimum train length. This is of vital importance when considering elements like platform and siding lengths, passing loops on single-track sections, and fiddle-yard dimensions.

Indeed, a golden rule to bear in mind at all times when planning your track design is one summed up succinctly in a chapter heading in C.J. Freezer's *Design Manual* as mentioned above – "The train is the key". In other words, you must first decide on the maximum length of the trains you intend to run on

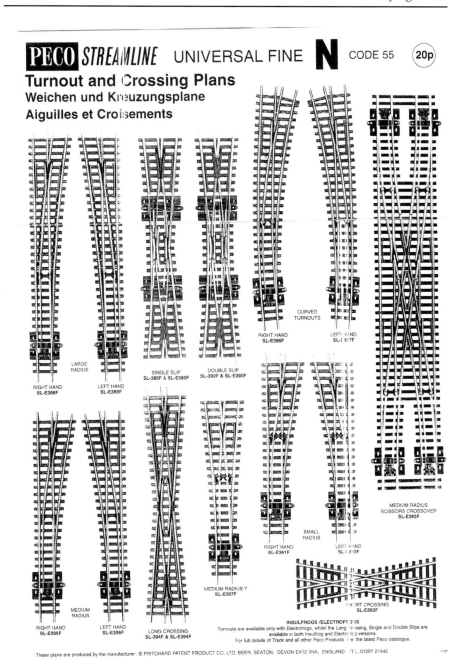

PECO *STREAMLINE* UNIVERSAL FINE **N** CODE 55 (20p)

Turnout and Crossing Plans
Weichen und Kreuzungsplane
Aiguilles et Croisements

CURVED TURNOUTS

RIGHT HAND
SL-E386F

LEFT HAND
SL-E387F

LARGE RADIUS

RIGHT HAND
SL-E388F

LEFT HAND
SL-E389F

SINGLE SLIP
SL-380F & SL-E380F

DOUBLE SLIP
SL-390F & SL-E390F

MEDIUM RADIUS
SCISSORS CROSSOVER
SL-E383F

RIGHT HAND
SL-E391F

LEFT HAND
SL-E392F

SMALL RADIUS

RIGHT HAND
SL-E395F

LEFT HAND
SL-E396F

LONG CROSSING
SL-394F & SL-E394F

MEDIUM RADIUS

MEDIUM RADIUS Y
SL-E397F

SHORT CROSSING
SL-E393F

INSULFROGS / ELECTROFROGS
Turnouts are available only with Electrofrogs, whilst the Long Crossing, Single and Double Slips are available in both Insulfrog and Electrofrog versions.
For full details of Track and all other Peco Products see the latest Peco catalogue.

These plans are produced by the manufacturer © PRITCHARD PATENT PRODUCT CO. LTD, BEER, SEATON, DEVON EX12 3NA, ENGLAND TEL 01297 21542

PLANNING AID . . Peco produce these useful sheets of actual-size turnout and crossing plans to cut out and place on your layout to assist in track design your layout, and then you can arrange your track plan accordingly. If you are proposing to build a branch-line terminus you can get away with maximum train lengths of a tender loco and two or three coaches and a tank loco and 8-10 wagons. For a main line, passenger formations of less than six coaches look wrong, except for local services, and goods trains should aim for a minimum of 15-20 small wagons or 8-10 bogie vehicles.

A BR Mk 1 coach in N Gauge measures around 6in (152mm) and express locos are about the same length, so a six-coach train will be 3ft 6in (1.4m) long. If you are modelling a main line or cross-country route, this should be the absolute minimum length of your station platforms. Whatever the minimum you decide on, you should add at least 10-15% to your layout dimensions to avoid the trains crowding out the track formation.

If you have the space and want to model prototypical full-length express trains, you should be aware that a 12-coach train plus engine adds up to almost six feet (1.8 metres) in length, and station platforms to accommodate it would need to be a minimum of six feet. Suddenly, N Gauge doesn't seem such a small scale after all!

Most freelance track designs start life as rough sketches of indeterminate scale but more detailed design work should be carried out on a sheet of paper laid out in a grid scale such as one inch to the foot or metric equivalent. Alternatively, if your are reasonably computer-literate, there are simple CAD (computer-aided design) programs available specifically designed for layout-planning which allow you to plot a design on your PC without recourse to a pencil and eraser.

The most sophisticated CAD aids can now allow you to produce a 3-D perspective view of your proposals and even include moving trains. On the downside, however, such CAD programs are of US origin and thus have a North American bias which can make it difficult to produce anything looking remotely like a UK location.

It is perfectly feasible to work from a scaled-down track plan of your own design or as published in a magazine or book, but unless you feel you can follow that plan's design and dimensions absolutely to the letter, you should try to produce a 1:1 scale plan in actual size if possible.

You can use decorator's wall-lining paper or the reverse side of off-cuts of wallpaper for this purpose, but a better choice is to use thick white art card as supplied in art shops. This normally comes in A2-sized sheets and by using a soft drawing pencil (easily erasable) you can not only draw in the actual track formation but also rough approximations of scenic elements such as roads and waterways and trackside structures such as stations and bridge locations. Peco provide sheets of actual-size printed copies of points to allow you to place these elements of your design in situ, as it were. Rolling stock can then be placed on

SPACE STATION . . . You'll need plenty of room to run prototype full-length trains, as seen on Daleside Parkway layout at the recent N Gauge show in Warwickshire (HF)

the track outlines to see how trains would actually look at any given location.

Some modellers even go to the trouble of building rough card outlines of actual buildings to place on the plan which can then be moved around until the most satisactory location is decided upon.

Finally, a few words about fiddle-yards will be appropriate here. Unless your layout is totally self-contained with everything on view at all times, you will need to build into your plan some form of "backstage" area which can be said to represent the rest of the railway network – or at least that part of it from which your trains reach the "onstage" display and to which they disappear again through that tunnel or behind the backscene.

The delightful term "fiddle-yard" was coined in the early days of model railways and is now used for any "off-stage" part of your track design in which you can add or remove rolling stock or re-arrange train formations by hand – a practice sometimes referred to as "crane-shunting". On a small branch-line layout with just a couple of trains, this could be as simple as a continuation of a single line to a buffer stop in the hidden area. But a "fan" of two or more sidings would be preferable – and the more stock you have, the more hidden on-track storage you need. More complex alternatives for terminus-to-fiddle-yard layouts are to install a traverser or sector plate or a cassette system in which individual trains are held in removeable sections of track. For continuous runs, you will need a series of hidden loops off your main line to hold ready-marshalled trains out of sight as well as giving you space to add or subtract locos or vehicles.

Don't forget that when drawing up your plan, you must include reasonable space for your fiddle-yard. The more expansive you intend your train operations to be, the more room you will need for this vital, but hidden feature.

OFF-STAGE STORAGE . . . this is a sector plate-style fiddle-yard in which the storage lines slide over to meet the double-track formation leading to the main layout area

6 A Firm Foundation

HAVING settled on a suitable layout plan and the intended era in which the model will be based, the time has come to turn that dream into a reality by actually building the proposed system. But you can't lay a centimetre of track until you have constructed the baseboard on which the trains will actually run.

There are two basic forms of baseboard construction – solid and open-frame. For simple layouts, particularly those on one level – and especially for raw beginners – conventional closed-frame solid baseboards are recommended as the techniques of construction are relatively simple and the end-result provides sturdy support on which track and scenery can be laid.

Most general books on railway modelling provide detailed instructions on baseboard building and two excellent books by railway modelling expert C.J. Freezer, *The Model Railway Manual* and *The Model Railway Design Manual*, originally published by PSL in 1994 and 1996 respectively, probably contain more valuable advice and instruction on this subject than you will ever need. Ian Morton's *Baseboards for Model Railways*, first published in 2007 in Ian Allan's *Aspects of Modelling* series, is also recommended for beginners.

These books are generally aimed at 00 modellers but the principles and practice of baseboard construction are broadly the same for any scale. N Gauge newcomers reading up on the subject may be tempted to think they can skimp on some elements of baseboard construction because 2mm scale models are so much more smaller and lighter than their 00 equivalents.

But while it is true that an N Gauge loco, for instance, is only one-eighth – by volume – of its 00 equivalent, the weight difference is usually a lot less because it is the motorised mechanisms that make up far more of the bulk of locos in the smaller scale. And in any case, baseboards should always be as sturdy as possible because when your layout is complete, the only elements that you'll want to see in motion are the actual trains!

Anyone who can put together a piece of flatpack furniture or tackle basic DIY jobs around the home should be able to construct a solid-top baseboard (as

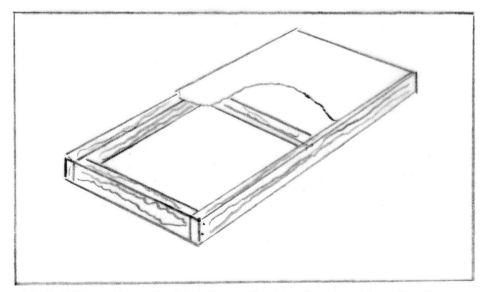

SOLID TOP . . . A basic 4ft x 2 ft (120cm x 60cm) baseboard module on 2in x 1in (50mm x 25mm) framing, covered in a sheet of chipboard, MDF or similar

illustrated above). Just a few basic tools are all you need – a tenon saw, a drill, a hammer, two or three screwdrivers, and a metal rule should suffice.

Baseboards are essentially composed of three interlinked elements – the framing, the top surface and the method of support. Only the most rudimentary carpentry skills are necessary to saw up the wood and then screw and glue together the basic framework with cross-bracing as shown.

For the top surface you can use chipboard, MDF (medium density fibre), insulation board, plywood or any other wood that comes in board form, although the first two are the most popular. The recommended maximum section size of 4ft x 2ft (120cm x 60cm) is exactly one-quarter of the size of a standard 8ft x 4ft (2440mm x 1220mm) sheet of wood, as usually supplied to DIY stores.

Chipboard is normally 15mm (0.5in) in depth. It has the advantage of being easy to work with but is relatively heavy, although bracing at 9-12in (23-30cm) intervals is recommended because it has a tendency to warp under extreme temperature fluctuations.

MDF – which can usually be found in hardware stores – is available in a wide choice of thicknesses but 15mm or thereabouts is the recommended choice for baseboards. It cuts relatively easy, even using a heavy-duty craft knife and is less prone to warping – unless it gets wet. But MDF is heavier than chipboard and when it is being cut it produces a fine sawdust which can be a throat and lung irritant – so a face mask is advisable. Both chipboard and MDF will not take

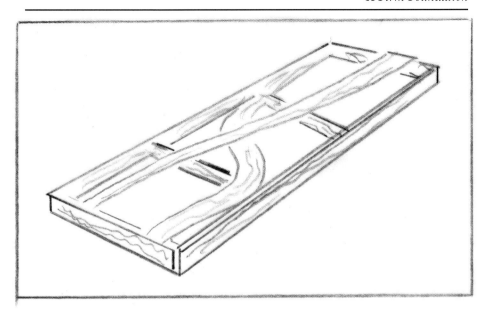

OPEN FRAMING . . . A similarly-sized module with plywood bases for the railway line and below-track river or roadway around which the scenery will be built

track pins easily without some pre-drilling. Some forms of insulation board are too light to be suitable for a layout without heavy framing, but a 9mm "hobby board" sold under the trade name Sundeala is ideal.

It is relatively light, easy to cut and drill, takes track pins easily, has a useful sound-deadening effect and needs only basic framing. It can be difficult to locate, however, as not all DIY stores stock it. See adverts in the modelling press or turn to their website www.sundeala.co.uk for more details.

Plywood is the most expensive of the four and also comes in various thicknesses with again 15-20mm being the best option. It is stronger still but less easy to work and more expensive. With plywood, it is better to glue down track on an underlay of cork or similar material.

The overall dimensions of your planned layout will depend on its location in the home, but unless it is to be free-standing with full walk-round space, the width should be no more than 3ft (1 metre), which is about as far as the average adult arm can stretch.

The best form of construction is by building baseboard modules which should be no larger than 4ft x 2ft (120cm x 60cm) and then linked together for erection. This is the largest unit which one person can carry or can be manipulated through corridors or doorways in the average house or shed.

The framework should be constructed from 2in x 1in (50mm x 25mm) softwood, stood on end, with cross-bracing at no more than 12in (300mm)

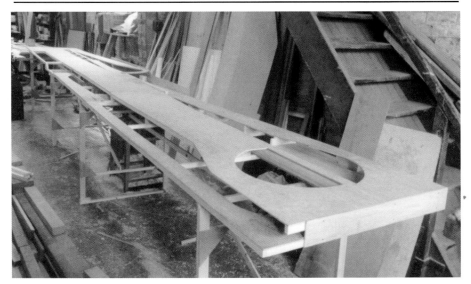

BIG PROJECT. . . This is the basic framework of Littlewood being constructed by master modeller Richard Deas. Not exactly a job for beginners, though!

intervals for strength. Simple glued and screwed butt joints will suffice, although more complex joints may be preferred if your carpentry skills are up to the task.

If you know the dimensions of your baseboard or modules when purchasing your base material, ask the hardware store or timber merchant to cut it to size for you. When erecting your layout, sections should be screwed and bolted together using coach bolts or something similar and also clamped for rigidity. Coach bolts have the advantage of being readily removable which will ease the task of dismantling sections of your layout should the need arise.

One other alternative worth considering for a ready-built solid baseboard that won't need any framing or cross-bracing is a plain household internal door as sold in DIY stores. These are ideal if you are planning a layout no bigger than 2ft 6in (0.75m) wide and 6ft 6in (2.2m) long, but if you have any other dimensions in mind, forget it.

Open-top construction is more complicated but the starting point is a framework similar to the above without the solid board on top. The frame itself should be stronger to compensate for the missing top-piece, using timber of 2in x 2in (50mm x 50mm) for the outside frame and 15-20mm plywood sheet for the cross-bracing.

The only solid part of the top section needs to be the track-bed, which should then be formed using pre-cut plywood sections to match the intended layout. Major landscape features such as rivers or roads can also be added as solid plywood sections before constructing the landscape. There are various ways of filling in the gaps between the track and the board edges on which the scenery can be constructed, as outlined further in Chapter 9.

The advantages of open construction is that you can add much more variety to the landscape, which can be an important element in a scenic N Gauge layout, by modelling both above and below the track level. A viaduct over a valley or river is only really feasible using this method. A disadvantage is that you must plan out your track diagram carefully before you start as once your track-bed sections of plywood are in place, there will be no opportunity to make anything but the smallest of adjustments.

It is certainly not advisable to use open-frame where you have complicated track sections such as at main-line station throats, although advanced modellers or those who are skilled at carpentry can combine both open and solid-frame elements in the same module with a little ingenuity.

It is also possible to allow limited scenic changes of scenic level such as under-bridges or water formations on solid baseboards by cutting out small sections – while remembering not to damage the basic framework.

The final touch for baseboards of all kinds which hasn't been mentioned yet is the method of support. Assuming your layout is not small enough to run on a shelf or a table-top, it will need legs to raise it off the ground. If the layout is to be permanently erected, than solid legs of at least 2in x 1in (50mm x 25mm) timber are needed at intervals of no more than 4ft (1.2m) with cross-bracing as in the

SOLID CONSTRUCTION . . Littlewood's complex framework shows the high standard of workmanship on this mammoth modelling enterprise undertaken by Richard Deas

main framework. Even better is 2in x 2in (50mm x 50mm) timber which needs less extensive cross-bracing and provides a more solid foundation.

Layouts can also be mounted permanently or temporarily on trestle-supports made from wood or metal which can be purchased in built or kit form.

One other point that often causes confusion with baseboards and has a bearing on the support is the ideal height. Assuming you – as operator – will be sitting down most of the time, the best height should be around kitchen worktop height – around 3ft (1 metre). If you prefer to stand while operating your layout, you may want to have it slightly higher.

If the idea of building your own baseboard fills you with trepidation, don't let that put you off the whole idea. The advertising pages of the monthly magazines contain regular adverts from specialist firms of builders who will construct a baseboard to your dimensions – or even the whole layout if you want. You can also purchase basic baseboard kits in modular form.

The American firm Woodland Scenics, a partner of Bachmann, produce a series of ready-made modules in various shapes and sizes which can link together to produce an endless variety of layouts under the Mod-U-Rail name. Their website also includes a host of track plans which are tailored to the modules. Mod-U-Rail is primarily aimed at US modellers and North American locations but there is no doubt that such a system could be adapted relatively easily to a UK layout and many UK traders stock Woodland Scenics products.

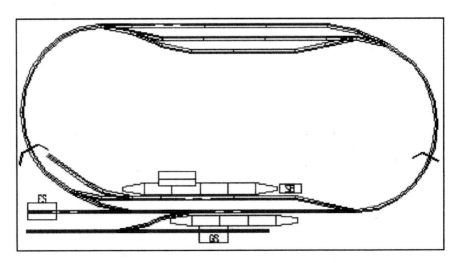

BRANCHLINE TRAIN SET . . . This 4ft x 2ft continuous run with passing loops and sidings makes a perfect starter layout and can be provided ready-built with 9mm MDF baseboard, Code 80 rail, power supply and scenic accessories by The Goods Yard. See their website www.thegoodsyard.co.uk for this and other customised N Gauge layouts

7 Making Tracks

NOW you've got your baseboard built, we are just a couple of stages away from getting those trains running! But the next stage in the layout construction process is in many ways the most important. To run trains, you need track, and to run trains efficiently and reliably, you need well-planned and well-laid track.

Worldwide, there are several manufacturers of 9mm-wide track in both sectional and flexible forms. But beginners, particularly modelling British outline, need look no further than Peco for almost everything related to your track requirements. The Devon-based company has been supplying N Gauge track for more than 40 years and a wide range of products are offered in three different but complementary formats.

The first thing that needs to be said about N Gauge track is that it is one of the least prototypically-accurate aspects of the scale. This is a regrettable but unavoidable consequence of the compromises necessary to provide a robust and flexible system of trackwork for the oversized wheels of N Gauge rolling stock to run on consistently and smoothly.

Indeed, if you could compare an item of N Gauge rolling stock sitting on a section of N Gauge track with its exact equivalent in real life, you wouldn't be able to escape the fact that the extremely oversized rails and chunky-looking sleepers of the model version are greatly distorted approximations of the real thing. Fortunately, we do not make such comparisons when considering our N Gauge models and when viewed from above, the small size of the track means that such distinctions become meaningless anyway.

Of the three alternative Peco formats, the sectional Setrack is the most straightforward to use and can be ideal for beginners with very simple layouts. It comes in preformed lengths in straight and curving sections with a basic range of points and the ends of each rail are fitted with track joiners – known as fishplates – which are simply pushed together. The advantage of this system is that you

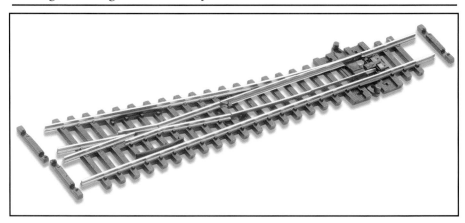

UNIVERSAL TRACKAGE . . .Peco is the name that many thousands of modellers turn to first. This is the Code 55 small radius right-hand Electofrog turnout . . .   (Peco)

can play around with various schemes before deciding on the settled result, but the main drawback is that you are limited in your design to the parameters of the various sections of track available – and only traditional wooden sleepering is made.

For all but the most simple layouts, Peco's flexible track is recommended, but it is important to realise at the outset that there are two varieties of this – Code 80 Universal Standard and Code 55 Universal Fine – both produced with traditional wooden sleepers and the modern concrete version. The code numbers refer to the actual dimensions of the rails – the original Code 80 uses a tall but narrow rail outline designed to accommodate the deep European-style flanges on early N Gauge products, particularly those produced by German

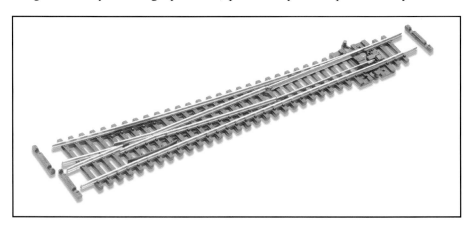

. . . and this is the Code 55 large radius right-hand Electrofrog turnout   (Peco)

manufacturers like Arnold and Fleischmann. British outline models were also designed to run on Code 80-style rail. Unfortunately, though, it can provide problems for US-manufactured N Gauge rolling stock which normally has less clearance under the body – leading to derailments on crossings – and also uses finer wheels. Peco responded to calls for a more universally acceptable design with Code 55, which has smaller rails which are moulded deeper into the sleeper base.

For British N Gauge stock, either version is perfectly acceptable and the difference between the two is virtually indistinguishable to the naked eye, particularly with the rails in situ. The success of Code 55 has effectively made it the new British standard for N Gauge track but the two formats sell side-by-side and there is no problem joining Code 80 to Code 55 track – or, indeed, either to Setrack – with the requisite Peco rail joiners.

Flexible track comes in 3ft (914mm) lengths and is slightly more difficult to handle than Setrack because it must be cut to the desired length and formation using a razor saw. The track must be held firmly – preferably clamped at one end at least – while sawing the rails and it is advisable to use a purpose-made track-cutting jig. These can be found in model shops, but you could easily make your own by cutting two rail-sized grooves 9mm apart in a small block of wood.

The plastic webbing that links the sleepers can then be cut with a craft knife and one or two of the plastic chairs that hold the rail will need to be removed. It is advisable to use a fine file to then buff up the rail ends before fitting a track joiner ready to link up with the next section of track.

Curves of almost any radius are possible and the array of points available is wider than Setrack with turnout dimensions of small (12in/305mm), medium (18in/457mm) and large (36in/914mm) radius.

How you fix your track to the baseboard – and it MUST be fixed securely – is dependent on your choice of ballasting. The simplest form of ballasting Peco track is to use the company's own tailor-made grey foam underlay. This comes complete with sleeper indentations in rolls for plain track and pre-cut forms for points and crossovers. You simply glue the track to the underlay and then glue that to the baseboard. Pinning down the track is still recommended – but much less pinning is required than with other methods.

The principal advantage of foam underlay, apart from ease of use, is that it provides an effect sound-deadening effect. But the main drawback is that it is less realistic than the alternative method and the track sits up higher, which you need to bear in mind when allowing for clearances for platforms, level crossings etc. You can disguise this to a degree when adding scenic details to the layout later. Foam underlay also tends to degrade over time – with a lifespan of no more than 10 years being the norm, depending on where in the home your

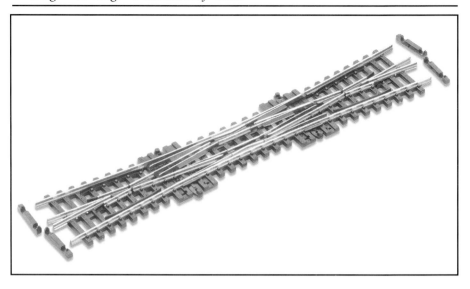

EVERY WHICH WAY . . . A very useful piece of Peco trackage where space is at a premium is this Double Slip which combines four turnouts and a crossing   (Peco)

layout is located. The main alternative to foam underlay is to pin the track to the baseboard and then to provide "loose" ballast. Novices should be aware that this is an incredibly messy and time-consuming process – and the bigger your layout, the longer it will take to complete!

However, when done well, loose ballasting can provide a realistic-looking formation as well as disguising the overscaled aspect of the track that was mentioned earlier.

Track pinned directly to the baseboard can lead to unacceptable levels of noise when operating trains, and most modellers who use this method prefer to fix a layer of flat 4-5mm thick cork sheet or similar material as a base before pinning and/or gluing the track to it. This is almost as effective a way of cutting the noise as foam underlay.

As loose ballasting is effectively part of the scenic element of your layout, this should not be attempted until all your trackwork and points are in situ and the formation and the electrics have been fully tested to ensure the track is level and all point mechanisms and operating systems are working as they should be. Loose ballast in commercial packs from model shops comes in a finely-granulated powder form and is available in differing grades and colours. Make sure you purchase only ballast that is clearly marked as being suitable for N Gauge as some varieties are over-scale for 9mm track.

You only have to look at colour photographs or film of real trackwork – or get out there and observe it with the naked eye – to see that railway ballast is never a uniform shade but can be a mixture of cream, orange, brown, grey or even black, depending on its condition and location.

Patience and care is needed when choosing and mixing shades of ballast and a great deal of trial and error may be necessary before a satisfactory formula is found for your individual circumstances. But that's all part of the fun – and a well-ballasted track formation can be one of the most satisfying visual elements of a completed layout.

The "tools" you'll need, ideally, are a small plastic sprayer of the sort sold in garden centres for indoor plants, a small receptacle to shake out the dry ballast on to the formation (an old pill bottle is ideal) and an eye-dropper or plastic syringe, plus some domestic washing-up liquid, a little water and some diluted PVA glue.

Having laid and pinned your track and fully tested it, your first task is to shake out the ballast mixture on to the formation at either side of the track and between the rails until it is just covering the sleepers. Then by gently tapping the baseboard alongside the formation with the handle of a knife or screwdriver, you'll find that the loose chippings will settle between the sleepers.

These can then be pressed down firmly using the end of a fine brush or other implement to ensure that the sleeper tops are clean. At the same time, use the same tool to build up a "shoulder" on the outside edge of the rail formation as in the real thing.

Fill the plant sprayer with cold water and then spray a fine mist of moisture over the ballast, from a height of no more than six inches, taking care not to get the track too damp. Adding a few drops of washing-up liquid to the water first will assist the "misting" process. Finally, mix a solution of one part PVA glue to three parts water, plus a few drops of washing-up liquid in the eye dropper or syringe and squirt this evenly and gently over the formation.

Take care when applying the glue not to touch any moving parts of points such as tie-bars or motors or any other electrical contacts and make sure you wipe clean the tops of the rails immediately.

It will take a few days for your ballast to dry out completely, depending on the layout's location. Once it's dry, you can use a small brush or car vacuum cleaner to remove any stray pieces of ballast from the formation but the task is not yet quite complete.

First, you may feel the need to touch up some areas of ballast with paint if they don't look quite "right" and then to give your track formation the finishing touch, you will probably want to paint the rail sides in rust colour, taking care again to wipe off any surplus paint from the top of the rails so as not to impede electrical pick-up for your trains. Only visible portions of your track need loose

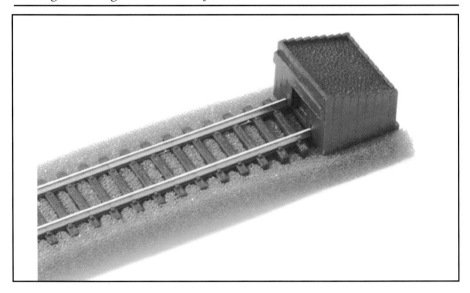

FOAM GUIDE . . . Peco produce a ready-made grey foam underlay complete with sleeper indentations which can be glued directly to the baseboard   (Peco)

ballasting and painting, of course, although hidden sections in tunnels and fiddle yards should still be laid on cork sheet or underlay to cut down noise.

As mentioned at the outset, extreme care must be taken when laying track, particularly at rail joins, over points, at baseboard joints and where there are changes of elevation, to ensure that there are no kinks or mis-alignments of height or breaks between rails. The small size of N Gauge means that a distortion of only a couple of millimetres in either dimension can lead to problems with derailments that could take forever to fix.

It is also important when laying curves in flexi-track to ensure that there is a smooth and gentle transition from straight to curve as too sharp a switch will be another likely cause of derailments.

On the subject of curves, one of the advantages of N Gauge – as mentioned earlier – is that you can turn a line through 180 degrees so that trains are running back in the direction from which they came in a space of around four square feet (two feet wide) with curves of 12-inch diameter. Such dramatic curves are completely un-prototypical and should only be used in hidden sections of the your layout such as tunnels and fiddle yards but so-called "dumb-bell" sections are a common feature of many N Gauge layouts.

On open sections of your layout, your curves should be restricted to a minimum radius of around two feet (0.6 metres) if possible. N Gauge track will actually curve as sharply as 9 inches (228mm) in diameter but this is not recommended as some stock would tend to de-rail on such a sharp curve. When laying curves, an invaluable set of tools is the Tracksetta sold in most model shops and many Internet outlets.

These come in fixed curves of six different measures from 9in (228mm) to 36in (0.9m) and also in a straight length. They enable you to pin down track with them in place while you work. For longer curves, you may find that purchasing two or three in each measurement will be a great help.

Another worthwhile accessory is a Six-Foot way gauge as made by Peco which will help you to check the accuracy of your alignments between tracks inch by inch as your tracklaying progresses. It can also be used to align platform heights correctly.

The most likely place for mis-alignments – if you are not careful – is obviously where two pieces of flexible track are joined, particularly on curves, and you should avoid rail joints at the exact point where a curve begins if at all possible.

Before moving on from tracklaying to the next important stage, electrics, mention should be made that there are several alternatives to Peco when puchasing trackage. Both Arnold and Fleischmann provide similar sectional and flexible N Gauge trackwork to match their Continental systems, as do Atlas and other manufacturers in the US.

Some of these products are not as widely available in the UK as Peco, although supplies can easily be tracked down over the Internet. Modellers of European or North American locations often prefer to match the track to the models designed to run on them.

One other track system gaining popularity for N Gaugers in the UK following recent articles in the modelling press is the Japanese firm Kato's Unitrack system, which is readily available in the UK from a couple of major traders.

This is a set-track system but with a form of built-in ballasting which gives the track an extremely robust but chunky appearance. Unitrack is easy to erect and dismantle again and again as it was designed as a table-top "train set" style system for Japanese homes where space is at a premium.

The comprehensive range of straight and curved sections – in three different radii – also includes pre-formed viaduct sections, stations, feeder tracks and even a special 62mm "conversion" track to link Unitrack to other makes.

It would be difficult, but not impossible, to disguise the toy-like formation if using Kato on a conventional layout but the ease of use and reliability of the system make it an interesting alternative. Unitrack also incorporates such useful innovations as ready-wired points, double-track formations, automatic lifting-barrier level crossings, road crossing tracks, automatic signals and magnetic uncouplers.

8 Switching On

AFTER track-laying, fixing up the electrics is the next most daunting prospect for the novice railway modeller with only basic knowledge of the subject. Even hobbyists who are on their second or third layouts will tell you that the whole subject of providing power for the track, points and ancillary items can be a minefield of complexity. However, please don't let tales of doom and gloom put you off!

Leaving aside for a moment the possibility of using the chip-based system of Digital Command Control (DCC), the method of powering a model railway layout with conventional two-rail wiring is, at the fundamental level, actually very simple.

All you really need to know is that N Gauge locos, as with other scales, run on 12-volt direct current (dc) using small permanent-magnet motors consuming up to one-amp of current, and the motion and speed are controlled by regulating the actual voltage reaching the motor and the direction of travel by altering the direction of current flow.

To do this you need a transformer to convert the mains voltage from 240 volts of alternating current (ac) to 16volts ac, a rectifier to change the 16v ac to 12v dc and a resistance control mechanism – better known as a speed controller – to vary the dc output in order to start and stop your loco and "drive" it at different speeds. This might all sound a bit scary to the newcomer but don't be discouraged – most basic proprietary controllers on the market achieve all three tasks in a sturdy little insulated metal box with a minimum of switches and knobs.

Some of these integral cased controllers have a centre on-off control knob in which the direction of switching controls the direction of the train, while others have a separate reversing switch, but that is essentially the only difference between them. They usually also contain a safety cut-out device which will automatically protect both locos and your electrical wiring from a power overload or short circuits.

Integral controllers can have up to four separate speed controllers allowing you to operate up to four trains – on different circuits – simultaneously, but a single or twin-speed version will probably suffice for the newcomer. Most units also have an auxiliary circuit of 16v ac terminals for controlling electrical accessories such as point motors, but you can also wire these up separately through stand-alone control boxes.

An important development of the basic control mechanism in the late 1970s was the introduction of the transistorised feedback controller which usually calls for an input of 15-18 volts ac and incorporates "pulse power" – feeding the energy to the track in short bursts rather than a constant stream. This is much more efficient as less "waste" energy is dissipated as heat and the "pulses" of power permit much more accurate low-speed running with less chance of stalling and smoother acceleration and deceleration.

There are several reputable and respected specialist manufacturers of control equipment whose products can be wholeheartedly recommended to the beginner, including Gaugemaster.

The two-rail system uses each rail of the track – via the powered loco wheels – as the two halves of the electrical circuit so the current flows from the controller through one track into the loco motor, and out via the other track and back to the controller. To achieve this, the powered wheels on one side of a motor are electrically insulated from those on the other side, and thus the current has nowhere else to go.

Assuming that track, wiring, electrical connections and locos are all assembled correctly, the two halves of the system should be completely insulated from each other throughout the layout and – hey presto! – you can start running trains!

As mentioned, there are several types of model railway dc controllers on the market and while each has its adherents, they all operate in the same basic way. They have a mains input lead (or connection point) and two output leads, normally marked with a plus (+) sign and coloured red, and a minus (–) sign and coloured black.

To wire up your layout, you need to take the current from the + terminal to one rail of the track (this is the "feed rail") and link the minus terminal to the other rail (which becomes the "return"). You can connect the power input and output wires to the track by using a proprietary connecting clip, as made by Peco, or by soldering the wire to the rail. The loco mechanism then collects the feed to turn the motor, completing the electrical circuit by expelling the current through the return rail.

That is a basic outline of what happens – and the beauties of the two-rail system are that it is essentially uncomplicated, reliable, safe and easy to use.

As the illustration below demonstrates, the position of your electrical feed is crucially important and is dependent entirely on your chosen track design. For the most basic layouts such as a small branch-line terminus or a simple continuous run as illustrated, just one power input point is needed. However, it is impossible to accommodate more than one loco on your layout at any one time with such a rudimentary electrical system and all pointwork must be insulated and aligned with the "heels" facing the feed for any sidings to be brought into play.

The next step is to break up your layout into isolated electrical sections in which separate feeds are supplied to each section, controlled through a bank of switches interposed between the controller and the track. Electrically isolated sections are crucial where you install a crossover between "up" and "down" lines and for reverse loops where a permanent short circuit would be created otherwise.

The rail joiners which link pieces of track together actually come in two types – metal ones which conduct power across the join and plastic insulated ones which do not. Sections of running line such as main-line "blocks" – to borrow the official rail signalling designation – sidings and loco "lay-over" positions in engine sheds or stabling points can be isolated from each other using insulated joiners and from the direct electrical feed using a switch mechanism built into the wiring.

Naturally, the larger the layout, the more electrical sections you'll desire and the more wiring and switches you'll need to achieve maximum operating potential – and the more chance there is of things going wrong and the underside of the layout looking like a jumble of spaghetti if care is not taken.

Adding to this jumble will most likely be an extra wiring headache – the need to power up your points. At the most basic level, points – or turnouts, to give them the correct technical term – can actually be switched by flicking a trackside lever as supplied by Peco. While this might suffice for basic table-top operation, it is hardly prototypical to have a giant hand swooping down from the sky every time you want a train to change lines!

There are two other tried-and-tested methods of point operation, which involve switching the point from a remote position on the edge of the baseboard, one mechanical and one electrical. Taking the mechanical first, this is the wire-in-tube method in which a sliding thin wire inside a plastic or metal tube is embedded in a narrow groove in the baseboard – to be covered later by scenic elements – linking the point's switching mechanism to a miniature lever on the layout edge. By flicking this lever – just like a signalman doing the real thing! – the tiebars of the point flick over to switch the direction of travel.

KEEPING THINGS SIMPLE . . . A couple of electtrical feeds is all you would need to operate a basic branchline layout like John Spence's marvellous Ashcombe (HF)

The advantages of wire-in-tube is that the components can be purchased and assembled cheaply and if installed correctly, should give years of trouble-free use. The disadvantage is that the further the points are from the baseboard edge, the longer the wire needs to be, and unless the point is roughly parallel to the edge, you may need to install a miniature angle-crank mechanism to change direction.

The second method, as mentioned briefly when discussing track-laying, is to use a proprietary electric motor to activate the points mechanism. Peco provide a motor which clips directly underneath their own points and is simple and straightforward to wire up. You'll have to drill a hole in the baseboard to accommodate it, which is one snag. It can also be positioned alongside the point but this is not recommended as you will have to hide it scenically in some way. There are several other proprietary points motors on the market, and all work in the same basic way.

Each point motor must be wired separately to a bank of switches which, in turn, is linked to the mains supply by a separate feed from the mains. The more points you electrify, the more wiring you will need and it won't be long before that spaghetti look appears. Fortunately, layout wire comes in an array of different colours but it is important when fixing your wiring not only to use as many different colours as possible but also to clearly identify each wire and make a note of what powers what, perhaps by writing colour-coded labels and sticking them at the nearest point under the baseboard. This will make it easier for you to locate any faults or make changes later.

While this brief outline tells you almost all you need to know about linking power to your layout to get trains running, there is much more to the subject of conventional two-rail wiring and related matters than there is space for here.

Points, for instance can have either an insulated plastic or conducting metal "frog", which is the length of vee-shaped rail at the join where the tracks divide. Both "Insulfrog" and "Electrofrog" points – to use Peco's proprietary name – operate in the same way and can be used interchangeably anywhere on a layout. The insulated version is built thus so that sidings and crossovers become self-isolating dependent on which way the point is switched. As well as avoiding the possibility of a short-circuit which would happen if rails of opposite polarity came into contact, they greatly simplify the electrical feeds at these places. The drawback is that locos travelling over them can suffer a brief power loss as electrical pick-ups hit the "dead" plastic section, which can lead to stalling, particularly in slow-moving manoeuvres such as shunting.

"Electrofrog" points have no "dead" section with a full metal frog and automatically switch power to the positive or negative side depending on which route is set. As there is no unpowered gap to the frog, the chances of a loco stalling are minimised, but insulated rail joiners have to be used to break track up into sections at various places to simplify train control and to avoid causing a short circuit.

This means extra electrical feeds have to be inserted and even that simple branch-line terminus with a run-around and a couple of sidings would need almost twice as many separate electrical circuits as one with insulated points.

This all explains how to operate trains one at a time on your layout by switching in and out of sections. For double-track lines where you might want to operate two or more trains simultaneously, you will need a dual controller or two separate controllers for each of the running lines.

Another aspect of electrical wiring which hasn't been touched on thus far is the question of signalling. It is possible to wire up both old-style semaphore and modern colour-light signalling to work independently or in tandem with electrical "blocks" and points, but this is a specialist subject and readers should look elsewhere for more information on this.

The more complex your layout and hence the wiring, the more likely you'll

*START HERE . . . The three-part **Wiring The Layout** booklets in **Railway Modeller's** "Shows You How" series tell you all you need to know to power up a starter layout*

want to construct some form of control panel to bring all your electrical outputs and inputs into one easy place. This, too, is a specialised subject which can be tackled later once you have familiarised yourself with running and operating your layout.

The foregoing is intended only as a brief explanation of the whole process of wiring up a layout, not as detailed instructions on how to proceed, and newcomers are advised to consult one of the specialist publications available on this topic. For the beginner, the inexpensive three-part *Wiring The Layout* booklets produced by the *Railway Modeller* in its "Shows You How" series are heartily recommended for an inexpensive yet comprehensive introduction to all basic aspects of layout and point wiring.

General modelling books like Iain Rice's *Railway Modelling The Realistic Way* and Cyril Freezer's *The Model Railway Manual*, previously mentioned, also go into the subject of two-rail electrics in far more detail. Whole books could be written on the topic and indeed they have been – *The Complete Book Of Model Railway Electronics* by Roger Amos, first published by PSL in 1990 and subsequently updated, is probably the most comprehensive ever published, with more than 200 pages packed with specialist information on all aspects of model railway electrics.

Before moving on, however, it is time for a few brief words on the subject of Digital Command Control (DCC), a revolutionary different way of controlling model railways which is gaining increasing acceptance in 00 and other scales and has started to make inroads into the N Gauge world.

Instead of powering locos through a conventional dc controller via electrically-separate layout sections, DCC requires just one simple feed to the track with the power in each individual loco switched on and off via a separate computer chip embedded in the loco. Each chip is coded separately so that you power up a particular loco only when you key in that loco's unique identifier code on the control panel. Likewise, each point on your track diagram is fitted with a chip and is operated only when its unique number is keyed into your control pad.

DCC allows you to "park" or switch off any loco on any part of the layout and also permits the operation of more than one loco on your network without the need to worry about switching power between sections or sidings. It also allows for two locos to head away from or towards each other on the same piece of track. Yes – you could create head-on collisions if you so desired!

Advocates of DCC are always keen to point out that there are several other advantages over conventional wiring – such as the greater control of starting and stopping locos, overall speeds, and less chance of a loco meeting a "dead" spot on the track created by dirty rails or wheels.

As far as 00 is concerned, DCC is now firmly established as an alternative to the traditional system of electrics and locomotives in that scale are increasingly being made available with factory-fitted decoders or sold as "DCC-ready" in which a space is readily available for insertion of a chip.

In the last couple of years, manufacturers of N Gauge have come to recognise that DCC could be the coming thing in 2mm as well. Graham Farish and Dapol are both now producing locos which are advertised as "DCC-ready" and

AUTO-MAGIC . . . The magnificent Littlewood layout by Richard Deas was almost fully automated from this compact control panel over one of the huge storage yards

Bachmann, with their EZ command system, and Gaugemaster, under the name Prodigy Advance, have launched DCC systems aimed at the British modeller.

However – and this is a big caveat as far as N Gauge is concerned – there are as yet very few locos which are "DCC ready" and converting an existing layout to DCC or building a new layout but retaining older rolling stock would be problematical, to say the least.

As 2mm modellers who have experimented with DCC know only too well, the tightly-packed mechanisms of many existing N gauge locos from the major manufacturers make it very difficult to find space to fit a chip anyway.

Having said that, DCC's popularity in the larger scales is increasing by the month, and it is presumably only a matter of time before DCC-ready locos in N Gauge are as familiar to us as in 00. In Europe and North America, N Gauge manufacturers like Fleischmann and Atlas now routinely produce locos which are either DCC-ready or come factory-fitted with decoders.

It is not feasible to mix up DCC and conventionally-operated locos in the same operating session, but there is no reason why you couldn't run both methods separately in a dual-wired layout.

Before starting out in N Gauge, it would be folly to completely overlook the future possibilities of DCC – but for that starter layout, conventional two-way wiring should suffice for now.

9 Setting The Scene

SO far, the construction of a model railway layout has roughly paralleled the development of the real thing. The pioneering railway builders of the Victorian era found and planned their route, laid the track, provided the power source – steam engines – and then began operating trains.

But for the next stage in building a layout, creating the landscape in which those trains run, the process is completely reversed. In reality, the landscape came first and the railway builders had to find a way to push their rails through fields, hills, and urban areas with the least effort and least disruption of the terrain. More than 150 years later, surviving lines usually blend into the landscape so well that it seems they have been there forever.

But with a model, you lay down the lines first and then build the scenery around them. And the goal of the scenic modeller must be to emulate reality by creating a landscape – whether it is wild moors, traditional farmland or busy town or cityscape – where the rails appear to have been driven through virgin country rather than have that scenery merely slapped on top of your track plan.

Also, as far as N Gauge is concerned, it is important to realise that a simple fact of railway modelling's dynamics is that the smaller the scale, the more important the scenic element becomes.

For modellers in the larger scales, particularly 0 Gauge and above, it is the models themselves that take centre-stage and lineside scenery can be perfunctory or sometimes even non-existent. Even in 00, there are popular layouts on the exhibition circuit where running trains is the most important thing and the overall scenic look of the layout is very much secondary.

But if you take the scenery out of a 2mm layout, you are effectively left with a train set on a board. Yet the beauty of N Gauge-sized scenery is that even the smallest layouts can usually produce the illusion of a railway in the landscape rather than just trains going round and round or from fiddle-yard to station.

RAILS IN THE LANDSCAPE . . . Few home modellers have the space to create such realistic scenery as Littlewood offered – but what a magnificent vista opens up here!

Experienced N Gaugers sometimes take the landscaping element so seriously that they design their favoured terrain first and then fit the actual route of the line in afterwards. And where space permits, it is possible to design a plan in which the railway, while being the focus of a given location, sits snugly in the landscape, not crowding out the countryside or townscape features.

For some modellers, adding scenic elements to the layout is a tedious exercise in which corners are cut where possible and compromises readily made. To others, creating the scenery as a finishing touch to the model is an unalloyed joy where the opportunity is eagerly seized to "play God" by creating hills and valleys, woods and fields, plus distinctive landscape features like rivers, ponds and waterfalls and man-made elements like canals, roads and buildings.

This is the one part of the layout where design can be given free rein, particularly with "freelance" imaginary locations, and you can model your favourite scenic elements including bridges, viaducts, the village pub or perhaps a ruined castle or windmill. Also, the scenic side of the layout is the one element that you can continue to change, improve and add to throughout your layout's life as you see fit. Unless you are modelling somewhere completely flat like the Fens, you will probably want to include a tunnel or two, if only to disguise sharp curves where your track turns through 90 degrees or a complete U-turn. An alternative option at the point where your track disappears off into a fiddle yard is an overbridge with carefully-positioned backscene.

Creating model scenery is broadly the same in any scale and most general books of railway modelling are packed with detailed advice on almost all aspects. When constructing a layout, you will no doubt have had an image in your mind of how the finished landscape will look from the moment that you settled on your track plan, if not before. Certainly, much thought should be given at the planning stage on how the general topography will look – and construction of your baseboard should have taken any outstanding features, such as viaducts or river valleys into account.

Broadly speaking, as far as British layouts are concerned, even with imaginary settings, there are only two kinds of landscape, rural or urban – or a mix of the two – and you will have made your selection at the outset.

Within those two general headings, however, come a host of alternative

SIMPLE BUT EFFECTIVE . . . The little station, house and church on John Spence's Ashcombe layout ooze rural charm and evoke a golden age of railways (HF)

possibilities. For a rural or semi-rural setting, a layout based on the wild uplands of the Settle & Carlisle, Shap summit, the Peak District, wild Wales or the Highlands of Scotland will have a totally different look and feel to a layout based on the West Country, East Anglia, or the agricultural spread of middle England. A sleepy town station on a minor cross-country line will have few features in common with a main line layout built around a busy river estuary or seaside location like Dawlish Warren in south Devon.

For urban locations, there are even more different types of setting. An industrial centre, a busy loco shed or goods yard, suburban housing, a major terminus or through station, a small branch-line terminus – the possibilities are almost endless. You can even mix any or all of these elements in one setting if space permits.

There are also many rail-linked industrial locations which can add extra interest to a layout – or even be the main focus – such as docks, warehouses, quarries, coal mines, oil depots and other industrial plants such as breweries and dairies.

If you are modelling a particular station or location – even adapted to a personal interpretation through "modellers' licence" – you can study and photograph the real thing to get a feel for how your model should look. Even if you have opted for a freelance design, you will presumably have at least a rough idea of the sort of real-life location you are modelling, and again a field trip with camera or sketchpad can prove very helpful.

With landscape design, you should never forget that in real life it is the fall and rise of the land which determines where cuttings, embankments, viaducts and tunnels are built and not the other way round – so try to ensure that your design takes account of this basic rule at all times.

As mentioned earlier, even with solid-frame baseboards it is possible to cut out small sections to allow for the insertion of below-track features such as an underbridge carrying a road or waterway. Larger features such as viaducts are more problematical and are better suited to open-frame construction.

With solid boards, your trackwork will probably be perfectly flat and then it is simply a matter of building up undulating sections alongside using one of several tried-and-trusted methods, such as shaped polystyrene blocks, papier mache, chicken wire, plastic netting, plaster-soaked bandage or even cut-up sections of old sheets or net curtains.

Polystyrene will be familiar to most modellers as the white foam-like pre-formed blocks that come as packing material with TVs and other household items, but the material is also available commercially in sheet form. Its advantage is that it is very light but sturdy and cuts easily using a small saw or carving knife. Its principal disadvantage is that the sawn edges crumble easily,

BRIDGING THE GAP . . . This magnificent GWR viaduct is a central feature of Claydon, a Cotswolds branch layout at the 2008 Warwickshire N Gauge show (HF)

and hence it can make a lot of mess. A hot-wire cutting method is available that slices through the material leaving much less mess.

By glueing sections together and using plaster-based filler to eradicate cracks and joins, an effective undulating landscape can be created easily, which can then be painted and grass scatter or other materials added. Specialist firms produce a a wide range of different materials to add bushes, walls, fences, hedgerows and the like to complete your chosen landscape. The beauty of this aspect of the model is that you can build up the landform by trial and error over a lengthy period of time while at the same time running trains.

With the papier-mache method, you can use either crushed-up paper or wood off-cut blocks to form a base over which inter-lacing strips of thick card – such as cut-up cereal packets – are fixed between the backscene board and the baseboard and then papier-mache pressed on to form the top surface.

For those of you unfamiliar from primary school days with papier-mache, it is made by tearing waste paper into small fragments and then soaking them in a mixture of wallpaper paste and water and mashing them by hand or with a spoon until they become a pulp. You then drain off the excess liquid and hand-mould the pulp to build a complete shell which, when dry, is then painted etc. This is also very light but easily damaged so care must be taken, particularly on portable layouts.

Both these methods are only suitable for solid baseboards, The third alternative, which can be used on either solid or open-top boards, is to use small sections of chicken wire or similar material which is pinned to the backscene and track sections and covered in plaster. Chicken wire – the hexagonal-pattern wire mesh originally designed for chicken coops – can be found in some DIY stores and garden centres and comes in rolls which can be cut to length.

A small layout won't need much so try to obtain offcuts from somewhere if you can. Its advantage is that it is stiff enough to be self-supporting over a width of 18in or more, which means less under-framing is needed, and it can be twisted into almost any required shape before being secured, preferably using a staple gun. A drawback is that cutting the wire will leave sharp edges which can cause nasty injuries if you don't take extreme care. You also have to ensure when adding the top covering of plaster or other material that you make it thick enough to avoid the hexagonal shapes of the mesh showing through.

Model shops sell various kinds of plaster for constructing scenery but there is no reason why you can't use a proprietary decorating aid like Polyfilla, which is slow-setting and relatively cheap. Plaster-impregnated bandage is the material used in hospitals for making plaster casts. It is sold in small packs under various names for model use. When dry, it produces a hard-shell scenic base over a support of crumpled newspaper or card strips.

A newer, but more expensive, method worth investigating is the SubTerrain system produced by the US firm Woodland Scenics, which uses pre-formed plastic foam sheets which can also be used to form the trackbed on open-frame baseboards.

It is impossible to say whether any of these methods are better than any other, and you can mix and match as your circumstances dictate. For cuttings and tunnel mouths, dried tree-bark – suitably painted – makes a very effective rock formation, and this material is readily available commercially.

Model shops, general modelling books and modelling magazines can provide much useful advice on specific elements of model scenery, such as trees, watercourses and roads. It is assumed that you will be dressing your model, scenically speaking, in summer mode – that is, with trees of full green leaves – if only because the vast majority of layouts are constructed in such a way.

But there is no reason why you can't set your layout in winter if you so choose, with bare trees and ploughed fields and frozen watercourses. You can even cover your landscape in snow. Some layouts on the exhibition circuit in recent years have featured wintry scenes and they are an interesting alternative.

SCENIC BREAK . . . This modern-day village scene with a busy road threading traffic past the church and pub covers a tunnel entrance on Daleside Parkway   *(HF)*

No matter what your chosen location, unless you have modelled a simple continuous run with no fiddle yard, at some point there will be a scenic break where the on-view section of your track disappears into the hidden section where you marshal your trains and switch rolling stock. A tunnel is the simplest device to send trains off on to the rest of the railway network, but overbridges covering simple holes in the backscene can do the same job.

The backscene is another important element of the scenery – to give the allusion that your layout does not have an abrupt rear edge but somehow disappears into the distance along the eyeline. Experienced artists can create their own backscene to blend in with trees or buildings set against the rear, but there are many excellent proprietrary backscenes available from Peco and other manufacturers.

While on the subject of tunnels, don't forget that when creating such hidden sections it is important to allow access space of at least a hand's width to rescue that recalcitrant rolling stock which will insist on derailing inside – and it will almost certainly happen! This can be created by a hole under the baseboard, from the side or rear, or even a removal top section.

The inclusion of other structures in your layout such as lineside buildings, farmhouses, churches, shops or whatever will depend on the location modelled. As well as the wide range of ready-painted Lyddle End structures now available from Hornby and Scenecraft from Bachmann-Graham Farish, there are many other manufacturers of N Gauge buildings both ready-made and in kit form, painted and unpainted, in card or cast resin.

All the books on general railway modelling already mentioned contain far more information about constructing scenery and adding the finishing touches to your layout. There are also specialist volumes available such as *Landscape Modelling* by Barry Norman (Wild Swan).

As the advertising pages of the monthly magazines readily indicate, there is a complete imdustry of firms large and small providing models of every description in kit-form and ready-built to decorate your landscapes.

In addition, accomplished modellers can use basic building materials such as plasticard to scratchbuild unique models or produce detailed scale copies of prototypes.

RACING THROUGH. . . A working lifting-barrier level crossing adds a contemporary scenic touch to Littlewood as an HST passes a train on the nearby preservation line

10 The World Of N

WHILE N Gauge modelling of the UK scene past and present offers a multitude of options for layouts covering the last 60 years or so, there is no reason why the 2mm modeller utilising commercially-available products needs to stick to a British outline subject.

As our potted history of N Gauge modelling in Chapter 2 showed, the scale first took off in a big way in Europe and it is the inter-linked national rail systems of the major European nations that offer the greatest variety of liveries and rolling stock for the 2mm modeller today.

The German, Italian, Swiss, Dutch, Belgian, French and Spanish railway systems from the 1950s onwards are covered reasonably comprehensively from manufacturers such as Fleischmann, Arnold, Bachmann, Marklin, Lima, Jouef, Minitrix, Rivarossi and Kato, while manufacturers of scenic accessories like Faller, Kibri, Noch and Preisler also abound. The European railway network embraced diesel power and electrification earlier and much more extensively than BR, so modern forms of traction predominate, but several of the most iconic pre-war and post-war steam loco classes from the major European networks can also be found in N Gauge.

One of the principal delights of modelling a European location is the fact that express trains rarely stop at a country's borders and hence you can run rolling stock of two or more different systems intermingling perfectly legitimately, especially if you choose to model a location – real or fictional – on one of the Continental mainland's major west-east or north-south through routes.

Particularly popular with modellers – as many an exhibition visit will show – are Alpine locations, both because of the scenic possibilities of mountain tunnels, spirals and spectacular viaducts and the fact that major Alpine through lines could carry as diverse a range of stock as anywhere on the Continent.

Several of the major European N Gauge manufacturers produce their own track systems. Fleischmann, under the Piccolo name, produce a ready-ballasted 9mm track which bears similarities to Kato's Unitrack as previously mentioned.

The history of model railway manufacturers in all gauges both in the UK and abroad throughout the 20th Century and into the 21st has been one of takeovers, mergers, bankruptcies and reorganisations. The British-based Hornby group now owns Jouef, Lima, Arnold and Rivarossi under the Hornby International banner and a visit to their website at www.hornbyinternational.com is a good starting point for anyone contemplating an N Gauge model set in Europe.

Much valuable information can also be acquired from any issue of Peco's monthly magazine *Continental Modeller* and there are also regular Euro modelling supplements in *Model Rail*.

North America, too, has its adherents as the basis for layouts with scenic attractions far removed from the UK scene such as semi-desert locations, the Rocky Mountains or busy urban and industrial settings. Perhaps the biggest manufacturer of North American N Gauge is Atlas, which features a wide range of diesel locos and rolling stock in the colours of many different railroads, both existing and historical, including Amtrak, Santa Fe, Union Pacific, Con-Rail, Delaware & Hudson, Grand Trunk, Penn Central, Northern & Western,, CSX

ALPINE SETTING. . . The Trisannabrucke bridge on a line linking Switzerland and Austria as recreated in N Gauge at the Warwickshire show in September 2008 (HF)

GO WEST . . . Oceanside, seen at the 2008 Warwickshire show, is set on the California coast and features long freight trains and Amtrak expresses in a rugged setting (HF)

and Canadian Pacific. Atlas also produce two kinds of 9mm track, the traditional Code 55 and the newer True-Track, which is a set-track system with a ballast base like the Japanese Kato, plus accessories including working colour-light signals.

Lifelike is another major manufacturer of North American N Gauge, as is Kato and Graham Farish's parent group under the Bachmann Spectrum and Bachmann Classic ranges.

For anyone interested in modelling North American railways, there are three US-based periodicals worth checking out. The monthly *Model Railroader* covers all scales while the bi-monthlies *N-Scale* and *N Scale Railroading* are 2mm-specific.

Finally, we must not overlook the Japanese rail network as a suitable basis for an N Gauge model. N Gauge is actually the most popular gauge for modellers in Japan because of the smaller dimensions of the average house there, and Kato and Tomix are the principal manufacturers. As the Japanese railway system was originally standardised on 3ft 6in gauge, many Japanese N Gauge models are actually built to a scale of 1:150, which is smaller than the European standard but slightly bigger than the UK dimensions. The world-famous Shinkansen "bullet trains", however, run on standard gauge track and are modelled at 1:160. Tomix, the railway division of the giant Japanese Tomy toy company, produces a wide range of Japanese outline diesel and electric locomotives, rolling stock and EMU/DMU sets, including an extensive range of "bullet trains", plus trackwork and scenic items.

As an interesting sideline, Tomix also produce a series of N Gauge Thomas The Tank Engine sets which are frequently hard to obtain in the UK but are highly prized by modellers wanting to add a quirky touch to their layouts for the amusement of young relatives and friends.

Kato has already been mentioned in Chapter 6 as a manufacturer of the robust Unitrack system and as a manufacturer of North American and European outline diesels and electrics, but it also, naturally, makes many Japanese locos and multiple-units, including various Shinkansen sets. Kato is also important to modern-day UK modellers as the manufacturer of Channel Tunnel Eurostar sets.

A third firm worth looking at for in Far East modelling is MicroAce, which produces the largest range of Japanese steam locos as well as diesels and electrics, although it should be pointed out that they prefer to market their products as sets (loco plus train) and do not sell individual items.

One problem with sourcing information on Japanese models is the language barrier – although a trawl of the Internet will quickly bring up a few useful English-language sources of information on what is available. The full range of Kato products are stocked by M.G. Sharp Models of Sheffield, a familiar name on the exhibition circuit, while the "Plus Daughters" business – www. plusdaughters.co.uk – are mail order specialists in European, North American and Japanese N Gauge as well as the UK scene. Check out also Japanese specialists www.jtrains.com.

An up-to-date overview of the Japanese modelling scene can also be obtained from www.japanese-model-supplies.com, a website run by an Australian mail-order firm which describes itself as "the first and still the only Japanese-only model specialist outside Japan".

As the name suggests, they sell model cars, dolls, robots, plastic kits and radio-control items as well as railways, but they specialise in the full range of Japanese N Gauge. Through their website you can also find the *Japanese Model Train Newsletter,* which is intended to provide all the latest news on Japanese N Gauge – in English – as soon as it is announced in Japan.

Apart from those mentioned, there are several other model railway traders in the UK who specialise in Continental, North American and Japanese railways in N and other gauges – and any issue of Peco's *Continental Modeller* will show you a veritable feast of products from around the world.

11 Running Trains

SO you've finally finished building your model layout, the scenery is sorted and you're ready to play The Fat Controller and run some trains. For most model railway enthusiasts, the achievement of the dream is that long-awaited time when you can sit back and begin operating your completed layout, perhaps as a welcome form of relaxation after a hard day at work. But the question might now arise about the most enjoyable way of doing that.

Initially, at least you will probably be content to operate your stock in a random manner as and how you see fit. With a small branch-line terminus or end-to-end layout, the enjoyment will come from running trains in and out with no doubt a little light shunting and marshalling of goods stock. Steam-era branches need only a good shed, cattle dock and perhaps coal bins for authentic goods yard operation and only two or three small sidings need suffice. The Arnold-style coupler and the small scale of N Gauge models don't make for good shunting layouts but specialist electro-magnetic de-coupling systems as produced by Peco can turn 2mm shunting operations into as much fun as in the larger scales.

For continuous runs, it may well be sufficient just to let your trains run round and round a few times before switching over in fiddle yards or stations.

In either case, you will probably want to introduce as much variety into your trains as possible to keep the interest level high. The types of train you can run on a British steam or early diesel-period layout, depending on your design, could encompass premium express passenger services (with a restaurant car), Pullman services, sleeper trains, secondary expresses (which may or may not have dining facilities), cross-country stopping trains, suburban services, two or three-coach locals, excursion and special trains, DMUs, parcels trains, mixed goods, coal and other mineral trains (and empties), works trains and block goods services such as express box-van trains, oil tankers or even specialist

BRANCHLINE ACTIVITY . . . A GWR "Flying Banana" diesel towing a solitary milk tanker pauses to pick up passengers on John Spence's little Ashcombe layout (HF)

freight services such as Army transport trains carrying tanks and other vehicles on low-loaders.

The later BR diesel/electric era can include a similar mix of passenger services (with Mk 1, Mk 2, Mk3 or even Mk 4 coaches), HSTs, Voyagers, block coal hoppers (and empties), Freightliners, block oil tankers, and other specialist freight wagons such as bulk coal, chemicals or minerals.

The later BR Sectorisation period and post-privatisation introduced even more variety for modern era layouts and the cornucopia of colours and styles possible will be limited only by the depth of your pockets!

If modelling a European, US or Japanese network, similar broad spreads of train formations will no doubt be available, depending on your chosen location and period.

After a time, however, simply watching the trains go by may begin to pall, and it is at this point that you may turn to the idea of some form of structured operation to add interest to operating sessions by devising a timetable or running sequence. With a layout modelled on a prototype, a timetable based on the original might be favoured, assuming you can track one down, or an imaginary

SPECIAL FREIGHT . . . A Virgin "Thunderbird" heads a trainload of logs past track workers on the modern-image Daleside Parkway at the 2008 Warwickshire show (HF)

timetable based on the supposed location at your favoured time period.

The terminus-to-fiddle yard layout lends itself best to timetable or fixed-sequence operation but a continuous loop of single or double track can also be operated in this way, even if seeing the trains go round and round is your principal enjoyment of the layout. You could, for instance, decide that a fixed number of laps per train was a "normal" sequence, with some or all of the laps stopping at the station, if you have one as the layout focus. A little imagination is required here, admittedly, but for these purposes your station could actually represent several stations on your main line or cross-country through route.

In any case, to many modellers there is much satisfaction to be gained just from watching a train of near-prototypical length travelling round your continuous run at scale speeds. The eye will tend to watch the loco and its trailing stock as they traverse your layout and with this limited field of view the repetition of the scenic elements play only a transitory role.

If modelling a specific location and time period, you will, no doubt, want to operate a range of passenger and goods services which as near as possible replicate the real thing. For present-day layouts, actual timetables or personal observations will help to formulate a pattern of train movements. For older settings, research through books and/or magazine articles will be necessary.

But for an imaginary layout, you can make your running sequence as simple or as complicated as you want depending on your mood, and, of course, on the stock you have available.

For sequence operation, some modellers use a series of numbered index cards on which each and every train movement, in order of operation, is delineated. Cards might say, for example:

No 12: 9.48 passenger train from X arrives in Platform 1.

No 13: 9.52 branch-line train arrives from Y in Platform 3.

No 14: 9.55 passenger train departs from Platform 1 for Z.

No 15: 10.02 branch goods departs from yard to Y.

No 16: 10.09 branch-line passenger loco detaches and moves to shed.

And so on.

Layouts at exhibitions are often operated in this fashion with two-sided cards on a flip-over loose-leaf binding mechanism. These have the dual advantage of reminding operators how the train sequence should unfold (on the operator's side) and informing spectators what they are seeing and what they can expect to happen next. An in-built advantage of a card system is that you can break off the

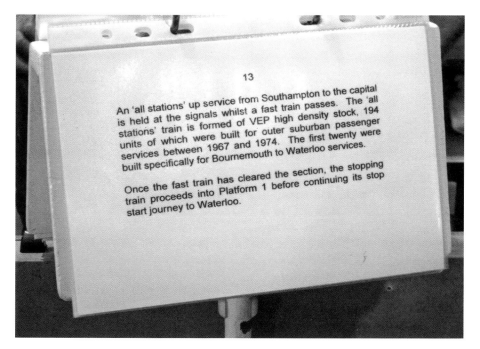

13

An 'all stations' up service from Southampton to the capital is held at the signals whilst a fast train passes. The 'all stations' train is formed of VEP high density stock, 194 units of which were built for outer suburban passenger services between 1967 and 1974. The first twenty were built specifically for Bournemouth to Waterloo services.

Once the fast train has cleared the section, the stopping train proceeds into Platform 1 before continuing its stop start journey to Waterloo.

THE NEXT TRAIN IS . . . This flip-over system kept viewers informed about all rail movements on the Bevois Park and St Denys layout at the Warwickshire show (HF)

sequence and pick it up again at any point without losing its internal dynamics providing you don't move the necessary stock around in the interim.

For timed operation, whether based on a real or imaginary timetable, don't think this means that you must run it in real time ie. waiting until 2.20pm, say, to send off a 2.20pm (1420) departure. It merely means that you run your trains in order of the timetable of services as they would appear in the real world, with or without a fixed ratio reduction built into your schedule. For one thing, running on real time, particularly on a branch line system, would soon prove incredibly tedious as in the real world there could be HOURS between train movements. As far as operating your model railway is concerned, you should consider that time in a 2mm scale world shrinks in the same way as other dimensions.

When operating your trains, whether on a sleepy country branch or high-speed main line, you will presumably want to adopt a scale speed. N Gauge locos – even the smallest steam tank engines – will run at the 2mm equivalent of up to 200mph with the controller turned up to full, which is plainly ridiculous.

But there is a relatively simple way to calculate scale speed. A scale mile in N Gauge is approximately 36 feet (10.5 metres), so if your train covers that distance in one minute, it is travelling at the 2mm equivalent of 60mph. This

SUPER-POWER . . . With freelance layouts like Littlewood you can run any trains you like – even Eurostar made regular appearances on Richard Deas's exhibition layout

ADDING COLOUR . . . Modern locos come in many different hues, like this Class 66 in the special blue/yellow livery of GB Railfreight/Medite from Graham Farish

is easy enough to calculate on a continuous run where you can work out the number of loops, or fractions thereof, which total 36 feet and then practise timing the train to run that distance in 60 seconds or thereabouts. If your loop is 9ft (2.7m) in diameter, for example, a 60mph train will take one minute for four consecutive loops.

On end-to-end layouts, working out scale speed is slightly more complicated as you will need to time your loco over the the longest available run. For 60mph you can break down the calculations so that 12ft (3.6m) is covered in 20 seconds, 6ft (1.8m) in 10 seconds or three feet (1 metre) in 5 seconds, for example.

Slower speeds can be worked out with the help of the following table based on the (approximate) distance a train travels on your layout:

10 mph is equivalent to 6ft (1.8m) per minute
20 mph is equivalent to 12ft (3.6m) per minute
30 mph is equivalent to 18ft (5.5m) per minute
40 mph is equivalent to 24ft (7.3m) per minute
50 mph is equivalent to 30ft (9.1m) per minute
60 mph is equivalent to 36ft (10.5m) per minute

It is even possible to buy digital speedometers which will give an accurate read-out of the scale speed of any train on your layout, while experienced modellers sometimes opt for special speeded-up clocks to give operating sessions that extra feeling of authenticity.

Of course, you don't have to keep exactly to a particular scale speed when

FLYING THE FLAG . . . No modern-day main-line layout would be complete without a container train. This 63ft bogie wagon with its P&O load is from Graham Farish

running your trains – only a pedantic perfectionist would argue that that is 100% necessary. But it is as well to appreciate just what is involved in keeping your running sessions within the parameters of a scaled-down reality.

As far as timetabled operation is concerned, it is possible – without going too deeply into the mathematics involved – to scale down model time to a fixed ratio of, say 12:1. This would mean that five minutes of actual time in the model world equates to one hour in reality. In this way, you could in theory run a full 24-hour sequence on your layout in a single operating session of no more than two hours – at least as far as main running is concerned. Paradoxically – and for obvious reasons – any shunting operations you add into the operating mix will run in real time, or an approximation of it.

For some modellers, it is the ongoing process of construction of a layout that is the principal interest and actually running trains can quickly pall. Then the likely solution is to store, sell or dismantle the fruit of their efforts and start all over again!

Another way to expand your modelling horizons is to join a club. For N Gauge modellers, the first port of call should be the N Gauge Society. It is true to say that N Gauge modelling in the UK would not have developed the way it has without the support and encouragement of this organisation which was formed in 1967 as Peco was producing its first 2mm scale wagons – and indeed the society was instrumental in settting the UK standards for the scale.

Not only does the society produce an excellent bi-monthly magazine and an impressive handbook, it also produces more than 30 kits to make all manner of wagons which either fill in gaps in the RTR range or provide much more accurate scale models. The society also operates a comprehensive mail order

21st CENTURY FREIGHT . . . The new Intermodal bogie wagons with 45ft containers from Graham Farish bring the "Freightliner" block train concept bang up to date

service for N Gauge accessories, and operates a series of area groups in most areas of Britain which in many cases exist as model railway societies in their own right.

The society also has a thriving "international" section, the World Wide Group, which caters for anyone modelling railways outside this country, of whatever age or period.

Also worth considering are two trade-run organisations for N Gaugers – the Bachmann Collectors' Club and the Dapol N'thusiasts Club. The former covers both 00 and N scale with a full-colour quarterly magazine bringing advance news of new products – and there are members-only limited editions in both scales of both locomotives and rolling stock.

The Dapol club also offers exclusive items, discounts on products, a "welcome pack" with special items and invitations to members-only open days at the Dapol HQ in Chirk, near Wrexham.

Alternatively or in addition, you can also join a general railway modelling club. Most major towns in the UK have a club and many have dedicated N Gauge sections. Clubs are invariably friendly and welcoming places for newcomers and members should be able to give you much valuable advice and help before during and after you have created a layout.

Many societies have their own N Gauge layouts either under construction or for operation at meetings and/or exhibitions and these will normally be larger and more extensive than anything you are likely to be planning at home.

As a member, you will be able to join in with this activity and run your own locos and stock on it. Clubs usually also have well-stocked libraries and some even offer full workshop facilities.

12 The Future . . .

THE N Gauge modelling scene in the UK does not stand still. In fact, more and more new products have hit the shops each year as this decade has unfolded – and there seems to be no let-up in the expanding horizons of what is, or will soon become, available to the 2mm modeller in terms of new locomotives and rolling stock.

One of the most glaring omissions from the proprietary range of British steam locomotives since British N Gauge's inception in the early 1970s has been the LMS Royal Scot 4-6-0, a class of engine to be found hard at work on all manner of trains throughout the main line system of the London Midland region in the 1950s and early 1960s – from Glasgow to Bristol, Holyhead to Leeds, Liverpool to London.

The Royal Scots have been staple fare in the catalogues of the major 00 manufacturers for years and there cannot be many modellers of this era and style of layout in 2mm who hasn't pined for a similar model in the smaller scale. Certainly, this writer's long-held fixation with modelling the Settle & Carlisle in its BR glory days has been the poorer for the lack of a ready-made 2mm version of a Holbeck-based Scot in Brunswick Green to haul the Thames-Clyde Express up the Long Drag to Ais Gill summit.

So Graham Farish's announcement back in the summer that the Fowler/ Stanier Royal Scot would be its next major release was naturally greeted with unashamed glee here and no doubt elsewhere – and it was an absolute thrill to see pre-production models on display on Bachmann's stand at the national N Gauge Show at the Warwickshire Exhibition Centre in mid-September.

If that wasn't enough to excite almost any steam-era N Gauge modeller, Dapol followed in the autumn with news that the BR 7MT Britannia Pacific -- like the 9F a former Hornby Minitrix product -- would be their "flagship" launch for 2009. Advance copies of their 2009 catalogue also contained news

MANOR BORN . . . Ixion Models' new GWR 4-6-0 is helping to set new standards for N Gauge steam locomotives in the UK. (Photo by Lindsay O'Reilly/Ixion Model Railways Ltd)

of a Southern Terrier tank loco, Class 67 diesels in EWS and Royal Train livery, the Class 58 diesel freight loco, Mk 3 coaches and DVT in various liveries and a Class 86 electric – plus 25kv catenary masts.

These announcements from the North Wales-based company come hard on the heels of their release of the LNER B17 "Footballers" – another class of locomotive that will be a welcome addition to the collection of many N Gauge modellers.

Mention has been made earlier of the Australian firm Ixion Models' production of a brand-new GWR Manor loco – and its official launch on the Dapol stand at the afore-mentioned N Gauge Show was an unqualified success. The locos – available in four variants in both GWR and BR guise – were being snapped up as fast as Ixion could produce them as pre-orders flooded in.

The success of the Manor's launch is particularly good news for British N Gauge as Ixion are now promising more innovative releases in the scale in the the next few years. They have already announced plans to capitalise on the Manor tooling with a model of the similarly-proportioned GWR Mogul in 2009, and Ixion director Phil Badger said at the Warwickshire show that they are looking to produce several other possible UK steam locos which are not available from other manufacturers – and it is a case of "watch this space".

As mentioned in Chapter 4, most BR and post-BR diesel classes have been released by Graham Farish and Dapol but there are a few intriguing gaps to fill in. Present-day DMU classes are now well represented by the 156 from Dapol in various liveries and classes 150, 158, 159, 168, 170 and 171 were all listed in the Graham Farish 2008 catalogue – plus of course the Class 220/221/222 Voyagers/Super Voyagers/Pioneers in various liveries -- but new DMU and EMU classes in various liveries are emerging all the time.

Another highlight of the Graham Farish display at the Warwickshire exhibition was the new Class 108 DMU in original BR green complete with those enigmatic "speed whiskers".

As far as steam locos go, it surely cannot be long now before we see BR Standard Class 4s and/or 5s in N Gauge, and what about the LNER/BR A1/2 express passenger locos – particularly following the recent launch of newly-built A1 loco 60163 *Tornado*? Southern fans would also love to see 2mm versions of the Lord Nelson and King Arthur 4-6-0s and the Schools 4-4-0s.

There are a host of other steam classes from all eras and regions which would be welcomed by many modellers – the GWR 28XX 2-8-0 Heavy Freight and Grange 4-6-0, the Southern N Class Mogul, the LNER K3/K4 and related variants, the LMS Fairburn tank and Stanier/Ivatt Moguls, and those unlovely but much-loved BR workhorses the WD 9Fs – to mention only a few.

The continuing re-modelling and re-branding of the privatised rail companies through sell-offs and exchange of franchises also keep the model manufacturers busy with new styles and liveries. Both Graham Farish and Dapol, for instance, wasted no time in announcing production of their Voyagers in new Cross-Country colours, while the Class 66 freight workhorse is now available from both companies in a variety of liveries alongside the original EWS red.

First Great Western have already worked their way through three liveries since privatisation while the recent demise of companies like GNER, Midland Mainline and Central Trains and various franchises re-modelled and re-born under the ownership of National Express, Stagecoach East Midlands, Arriva Trains Wales and London Midland all provide scope for new models or re-vamped versions of old favourites like the HST and various DMUs.

And come to think of it, now that Dapol are offering 25kv lineside catenary masts for 2009, does this mean that the Virgin West Coast Pendolinos could soon be on an N Gauge production line too?

All things considered, there is surely now no doubt that N Gauge modelling in the UK is entering a "golden age" where the scale can stand proud alongside 00 as its equal in both commercial and aesthetic terms.

What's holding you back? It's time to go modelling . . .

Index

ACKNOWLEDGEMENTS

THIS book has been in gestation for a long time! As a journalist with a life-long interest and enthusiasm for N Gauge model railways, I have followed closely the commercial development of British-outline 2mm modelling by Graham Farish, Peco and other manufacturers over the past 25 years or so – and it has been a puzzle to me that no one in that time has thought it a worthwhile task to put together a concise introductory guide to N Gauge for the beginner or, indeed, for anyone particularly interested in the scale.

Only after giving up a demanding full-time job and going freelance earlier this year has it been possible to find the time and the wherewithal to actually get my ideas down on paper (or computer screen!) at last.

This, then, is the N Gauge book that I have always wanted to read – and I have had to write it myself! Naturally, my hope is that others will want to read it too.

As a labour of love, the words are all my own – and I apologise in advance for any inadvertent errors of fact. I readily welcome any corrections, amendments, or – indeed – constructive comments via e-mail or letter (the addresses can be found elsewhere). My apologies, too, for a few rough line drawings that found their way into the book. I am no artist – and these were included only on the very few occasions where I felt that words or photos alone would not suffice.

No work of this scale can truly be a solo effort, of course, and I am indebted to several people for their help, principally with supplying images to accompany my text.

Thanks go first to Dennis Lovett at Bachmann-Graham Farish for kindly supplying me with so many wonderful images of GF products.

Also to C.M. Pritchard at the Pritchard Patent Product Co Ltd for supplying the requested Peco images, to the Dapol Studio in North Wales likewise, and to Lindsay O'Reilly and Phil Badger of newcomers Ixion Model Railways Ltd.

A special thank-you is particularly due to N Gauge master craftsman Richard Deas, who so generously supplied me with so many marvellous images of his wonderful Littlewood exhibition layout – which will be fondly remembered by many modellers.

I am also indebted to the modellers at the N Gauge Show at the Warwickshire Exhibition Centre in September 2008 who kindly let me photograph their work – especially John Spence. I trust my amateur efforts with a digital camera have not been a letdown.

Thanks, too, to Amanda and everyone at Rap Spiderweb for putting my dream into print.

Finally, I must thank Ian Foy for his technical advice and Adam Foy for his sterling work in producing several of the images you'll find herein.

Last, but by no means least, my thanks to Kate for putting up with my mood swings and helping to keep me focused on so many occasions when I feared this project was going off the rails!

HF October 2008

BOOKS AND WEBSITES

In compiling this book I have drawn on just about every book on model railways published in the UK in the past 40 years – mostly from my extensive collection. Many are now out of print and it would be a pointless exercise to list them all here.

There are several books I do heartily recommend – and you'll find these mentioned in the text (and index). I believe that most of these, if not all, were still in print at the time this book went to press.

I also mention a few N Gauge-related websites in the text but I have refrained from printing a comprehensive list of the ones I recommend and/or have used regularly. Anyone who can turn on a computer and navigate to Google can find all there is to be had by typing in the words "N Gauge" or "model railways" with a selection of key-words such as "traders", "forums", "advice" or something similar.

One website that does deserve a mention, however, is *www.ngaugesociety.com* – anyone in the UK who is contemplating an N Gauge layout should join the society forthwith!